Be Courageous

VICTOR BOOKS TITLES
by Warren W. Wiersbe

Be Loyal *(Matthew)*
Be Diligent *(Mark)*
Be Compassionate *(Luke 1–13)*
Be Courageous *(Luke 14–24)*
Be Alive *(John 1–12)*
Be Transformed *(John 13–21)*
Be Dynamic *(Acts 1–12)*
Be Daring *(Acts 13–28)*
Be Right *(Romans)*
Be Wise *(1 Corinthians)*
Be Encouraged *(2 Corinthians)*
Be Free *(Galatians)*
Be Rich *(Ephesians)*
Be Joyful *(Philippians)*
Be Complete *(Colossians)*
Be Ready *(1 & 2 Thessalonians)*
Be Faithful *(1 & 2 Timothy, Titus, Philemon)*
Be Confident *(Hebrews)*
Be Mature *(James)*
Be Hopeful *(1 Peter)*
Be Alert *(2 Peter, 2 & 3 John, Jude)*
Be Real *(1 John)*
Be Victorious *(Revelation)*
Meet Yourself in the Psalms
Windows on the Parables
A Time to Be Renewed *(daily devotional readings)*

Be
Courageous

Warren W.
Wiersbe

Though this book is intended for the reader's personal
use and profit, it is also designed for group study. A
leader's guide with visual aids (Victor Multiuse Trans-
parency Masters) is available from your local bookstore
or from the publisher.

VICTOR BOOKS®
A DIVISION OF SCRIPTURE PRESS PUBLICATIONS INC.
USA CANADA ENGLAND

In this book, Scripture references without book designations (e.g., 3:2; 7:5; 20:6) refer to the Gospel of Luke. All other references include the Bible book designations (e.g., Acts 3:5; 6:2; John 3:16), but where confusion may result, Luke references also include the Luke designation. References without chapter designation (e.g., v. 12 or vv. 2, 6-10) relate to the Luke passage under consideration in the study.

Unless otherwise noted, Scripture quotations are from the *King James Version*. Other quotations are from the *New American Standard Bible* (NASB), © the Lockman Foundation 1960, 1962, 1963, 1968, 1971, 1972, 1973, 1975, 1977; *The New King James Version* (NKJV), © 1979, 1980, 1982, Thomas Nelson, Inc., Publishers; the *American Standard Version* (ASV); and *The New Testament: An Expanded Translation* (ET) by Kenneth S. Wuest, © 1961 by the Wm. B. Eerdmans Publishing Company. Used by permission.

Recommended Dewey Decimal Classification: 228
Suggested Subject Headings: BIBLE, N.T.; LUKE

Library of Congress Catalog Card Number: 88-62852
ISBN: 0-89693-665-1

CONTENTS

Dedicated to
ERNEST and ANNIE LOTT
faithful servants of God
whose example and encouragement
have meant much to me and my wife
and to the ministry of Back to the Bible
around the world.

PREFACE

This book is a companion volume to *Be Compassionate* and takes Luke's account from chapter 14 to the end of his Gospel. In these chapters, we see our Lord steadfastly going up to Jerusalem to suffer and die. *Be Courageous* is not only a fitting title but also a fitting challenge to us in these difficult days in which we live.

Each of us has a "Jerusalem," a "Gethsemane," and a "Calvary" appointed just for us in the will of God. Like our Saviour, we must set our face "like a flint" (Isa. 50:7; Luke 9:53) and do what God has called us to do. It may not be easy, but it will bring joy to us and glory to God.

With this book, we complete the New Testament "BE" series that started in 1972 with *Be Real* and has continued through twenty-three volumes. The Lord has been gracious to help me during these busy years of ministry, and He alone gets the glory for any benefit these books have brought to His people.

I must add a word of appreciation to my wife, Betty, who over the years has done so much to protect my time and help me meet my deadlines. The staff at Victor Books has always been helpful and encouraging. Many people have told me that the "BE" series has been a blessing to them, and this has meant much to me. Thank you!

May the Word of Christ dwell in you richly and produce in you the fruit of righteousness that glorifies Him!

WARREN W. WIERSBE

Suggested Outline of the Gospel of Luke

Central theme: Our Lord's Journeys as the Son of Man
Key Verse: 19:10
Preface: 1:1-4

I. JOURNEY FROM HEAVEN TO EARTH—1:5–4:13
1. Birth announcements, 1:5-56
2. The babies are born, 1:57–2:20
3. Jesus' childhood and youth, 2:21-52
4. Jesus' baptism and temptation, 3:1–4:13

II. THE JOURNEY THROUGHOUT GALILEE—4:14–9:17

III. THE JOURNEY TO JERUSALEM—9:18–19:27

IV. THE MINISTRY IN JERUSALEM—19:28–24:53

1

The Man Who Came to Dinner

Luke 14

Sabbath Day hospitality was an important part of Jewish life, so it was not unusual for Jesus to be invited to a home for a meal after the weekly synagogue service. Sometimes the host invited Him sincerely because he wanted to learn more of God's truth. But many times Jesus was asked to dine only so His enemies could watch Him and find something to criticize and condemn. That was the case on the occasion described in chapter 14 when a leader of the Pharisees invited Jesus to dinner.

Jesus was fully aware of what was in men's hearts (John 2:24-25), so He was never caught off guard. In fact, instead of hosts or guests judging Jesus, it was Jesus who passed judgment on them when they least expected it. Indeed, in this respect, He was a dangerous person to sit with at a meal or to follow on the road! In Luke 14, we see Jesus dealing with five different kinds of people and exposing what was false in their lives and their thinking.

1. The Pharisees: False Piety (14:1-6)

Instead of bringing them to repentance, Jesus' severe denunciation of the Pharisees and scribes (11:39-52) only provoked them to retaliation, and they plotted against Him. The Pharisee who invited Jesus to his home for dinner also invited a man afflicted with dropsy. This is a painful disease in which, because of kidney trouble, a heart ailment, or liver disease, the tissues fill with water. How heartless of the Pharisees to "use" this man as a tool to accomplish their wicked plan, but if we do not love the Lord, neither will we love our neighbor. Their heartless treatment of the man was far worse than our Lord's "lawless" behavior on the Sabbath.

This afflicted man would not have been invited to such an important dinner were it not that the Pharisees wanted to use him as "bait" to catch Jesus. They knew that Jesus could not be in the presence of human suffering very long without doing something about it. If He ignored the afflicted man, then He was without compassion; but if He healed him, then He was openly violating the Sabbath and they could accuse Him. They put the dropsied man right in front of the Master so He could not avoid him, and then they waited for the trap to spring.

Keep in mind that Jesus had already "violated" their Sabbath traditions on at least seven different occasions. On the Sabbath Day, He had cast out a demon (4:31-37), healed a fever (4:38-39), allowed His disciples to pluck grain (6:1-5), healed a lame man (John 5:1-9), healed a man with a paralyzed hand (6:6-10), delivered a crippled woman who was afflicted by a demon (13:10-17), and healed a man born blind (John 9). Why our Lord's enemies thought that one more bit of evidence was necessary, we do not know, but we do know that their whole scheme backfired.

When Jesus asked what their convictions were about the Sabbath Day, He used on them the weapon they had forged for Him. To begin with, they couldn't heal anybody on *any* day, and everybody knew it. But even more, if the Pharisees said that nobody should be healed on the Sabbath, the people would consider them heartless; if they gave permission for healing, their associates would consider them lawless. The dilemma was now theirs, not the Lord's, and they needed a way to escape. As they did on more than one occasion, the scribes and Pharisees evaded the issue by saying nothing.

Jesus healed the man and let him go, knowing that the Pharisee's house was not the safest place for him. Instead of providing evidence against *Jesus,* the man provided evidence against the *Pharisees,* for he was "exhibit A" of the healing power of the Lord Jesus Christ.

The Lord knew too much about this legalistic crowd to let them escape. He knew that on the Sabbath Day they would deliver their farm animals from danger, so why not permit Him to deliver a man who was made in the likeness of God? Seemingly, they were suggesting that animals were more important than people. (It is tragic that some people even today have more love for their pets than they do for their family members, their neighbors, or even for a lost world.)

Jesus exposed the false piety of the Pharisees and the scribes. They claimed to be defending God's Sabbath laws, when in reality they were denying God by the way they abused people and accused the Saviour. There is a big difference between protecting God's truth and promoting man's traditions.

2. The Guests: False Popularity (14:7-11)

Experts in management tell us that most people wear an invisible sign that reads, "Please make me feel important"; if we heed that sign, we can succeed in human relations. On the other hand, if we say or do things that make others feel insignificant, we will fail. Then people will respond by becoming angry and resentful, because everybody wants to be noticed and made to feel important.

In Jesus' day, as today, there were "status symbols" that helped people enhance and protect their high standing in society. If you were invited to the "right homes" and if you were seated in the "right places," then people would know how important you really were. The emphasis was on reputation, not character. It was more important to sit in the right places than to live the right kind of life.

In New Testament times, the closer you sat to the host, the higher you stood on the social ladder and the more attention (and invitations) you would receive from others. Naturally, many people rushed to the "head table" when the doors were opened because they wanted to be important.

This kind of attitude betrays a false view of success. "Try not to become a man of success," said Albert Einstein, "but try to become a man of value." While there may be some exceptions, it is usually true that valuable people are eventually recognized and appropriately honored. Success that comes only from self-promotion is temporary, and you may be embarrassed as you are asked to move down (Prov. 25:6-7).

When Jesus advised the guests to take the lowest places, He was not giving them a "gimmick" that guaranteed promotion. The false humility that takes the lowest place is just as hateful to God as the pride that takes the highest place. God is not in any way impressed by our status in society or in the church. He is not influenced by what people say or think about us, because He sees the thoughts and motives of the heart (1 Sam. 16:7). God still humbles the proud and exalts the humble (James 4:6).

British essayist Francis Bacon compared fame to a river that easily carried "things light and swollen" but that drowned "things weighty and solid." It is interesting to scan old editions of encyclopedias and see how many "famous people" are "forgotten people" today.

Humility is a fundamental grace in the Christian life, and

yet it is elusive; if you know you have it, you have lost it! It has well been said that humility is not thinking meanly of ourselves; it is simply not thinking of ourselves at all. Jesus is the greatest example of humility, and we would do well to ask the Holy Spirit to enable us to imitate Him (Phil. 2:1-16).

3. The Host: False Hospitality (14:12-14)

Jesus knew that the host had invited his guests for two reasons: (1) to pay them back because they had invited him to past feasts, or (2) to put them under his debt so that they would invite him to future feasts. Such hospitality was not an expression of love and grace but rather an evidence of pride and selfishness. He was "buying" recognition.

Jesus does not prohibit us from entertaining family and friends, but He warns us against entertaining *only* family and friends exclusively and habitually. That kind of "fellowship" quickly degenerates into a "mutual admiration society" in which each one tries to outdo the others and no one dares to break the cycle. Sad to say, too much church social life fits this description.

Our motive for sharing must be the praise of God and not the applause of men, the eternal reward in heaven and not the temporary recognition on earth. A pastor friend of mine used to remind me, "You can't get your reward twice!" and he was right (see Matt. 6:1-18). On the day of judgment, many who today are first in the eyes of men will be last in God's eyes, and many who are last in the eyes of men will be first in the eyes of God (13:30).

In our Lord's time, it was not considered proper to ask poor people and handicapped people to public banquets. (The women were not invited either!) But Jesus commanded us to put these needy people at the top of our guest list *because they cannot pay us back*. If our hearts are right, God will see to it that we are properly rewarded, although getting a reward must not be the motive for our generosity. When we serve others from unselfish hearts, we are laying up treasures in heaven (Matt. 6:20) and becoming "rich toward God" (12:21).

Our modern world is very competitive, and it is easy for God's people to become more concerned about profit and loss than they are about sacrifice and service. "What will *I* get out of it?" may easily become life's most important question (Matt. 19:27ff). We must strive to maintain the unselfish attitude that Jesus had and share what we have with others.

4. The Jews: False Security (14:15-24)

When Jesus mentioned "the resurrection of the just," one of the guests became excited and said, "Blessed is he that shall eat bread in the kingdom of God!" The Jewish people pictured their future kingdom as a great feast with Abraham, Isaac, Jacob, and the prophets as the honored guests (13:28; see Isa. 25:6). This anonymous guest was confident that he would one day be at the "kingdom feast" with them! Jesus responded by telling him a parable that revealed the sad consequences of false confidence.

In Jesus' day when you invited guests to a dinner, you told them the day but not the exact hour of the meal. A host had to know how many guests were coming so he could butcher the right amount of animals and prepare sufficient food. Just before the feast was to begin, the host sent his servants to each of the guests to tell them the banquet was ready and they should come (see Es. 5:8; 6:14). In other words, *each of the guests in this parable had already agreed to attend the banquet.* The host expected them to be there.

But instead of eagerly coming to the feast, all of the guests insulted the host by refusing to attend, and they all gave very feeble excuses to defend their change in plans.

The first guest begged off because he had to "go and see" a

piece of real estate he had purchased. In the East, the purchasing of property is often a long and complicated process, and the man would have had many opportunities to examine the land he was buying. Anybody who purchases land that he has never examined is certainly taking a chance. Since most banquets were held in the evening, the man had little daylight left even for a cursory investigation.

The second man had also made a purchase—ten oxen that he was anxious to prove. Again, who would purchase that many animals without first testing them? Not many customers in our modern world would buy a used car that they had not taken out for a "test drive." Furthermore, how could this man really put these oxen to the test when it was so late in the day? His statement "I go to prove them!" suggests that he was already on his way to the farm when the servant came with the final call to the dinner.

The third guest really had no excuse at all. Since they involved so much elaborate preparation, Jewish weddings were never surprises, so this man knew well in advance that he was taking a wife. That being the case, he should not have agreed to attend the feast in the first place. Since only Jewish men were invited to banquets, the host did not expect the wife to come anyway. Having a new wife could have kept the man from the battlefield (Deut. 24:5) but not from the festive board.

Of course, these were only excuses. I think it was Billy Sunday who defined an excuse as "the skin of a reason stuffed with a lie." The person who is good at excuses is usually not good at anything else. These three guests actually expected to get another invitation in the future, *but that invitation never came.*

Having prepared a great dinner for many guests, the host did not want all that food to go to waste, so he sent his servant out to gather a crowd and bring them to the banquet hall. What kind of men would be found in the streets and lanes of the city or in the highways and hedges? The outcasts, the loiterers, the homeless, the undesireables, *the kind of people that Jesus came to save* (15:1-2; 19:10). There might even be some Gentiles in the crowd!

These men may have had only one reason for refusing the kind invitation: they were unprepared to attend such a fine dinner. So, the servant constrained them to accept (see 2 Cor. 5:20). They had no excuses. The poor could not afford to buy oxen; the blind could not go to examine real estate; and the poor, maimed, lame, and blind were usually not given in marriage. This crowd would be hungry and lonely and only too happy to accept an invitation to a free banquet.

Not only did the host get other people to take the places assigned to the invited guests, but he also *shut the door so that the excuse-makers could not change their minds and come in* (see 13:22-30). In fact, the host was angry. We rarely think of God expressing judicial anger against those who reject His gracious invitations, but verses like Isaiah 55:6 and Proverbs 1:24-33 give a solemn warning that we not treat His calls lightly.

This parable had a special message for the proud Jewish people who were so sure they would "eat bread in the kingdom of God." Within a few short years, the Gospel would be rejected by the official religious leaders, and the message would go out to the Samaritans (Acts 8) and then to the Gentiles (Acts 10, 13ff).

But the message of this parable applies to all lost sinners today. God still says, "All things are now ready. Come!" Nothing more need be done for the salvation of your soul, for Jesus Christ finished the work of redemption when He died for you on the cross and arose from the dead. The feast has been spread, the invitation is free, and you are invited to come.

People today make the same mistake that the people in the

parable made: they delay in responding to the invitation *because they settle for second best*. There is certainly nothing wrong with owning a farm, examining purchases, or spending an evening with your wife. But if these *good* things keep you from enjoying the *best* things, then they become *bad* things. The excuse-makers were actually successful people in the eyes of their friends, but they were failures in the eyes of Jesus Christ.

The Christian life is a feast, not a funeral, and all are invited to come. Each of us as believers must herald abroad the message, "Come, for all things are now ready!" God wants to see His house filled, and "yet there is room." He wants us to go home (Mark 5:19), go into the streets and lanes (14:21), go into the highways and hedges (14:23), and go into all the world (Mark 16:15) with the Gospel of Jesus Christ.

This parable was the text of the last sermon D. L. Moody preached, "Excuses." It was given on November 23, 1899 in the Civic Auditorium in Kansas City, and Moody was a sick man as he preached. "I must have souls in Kansas City," he told the students at his school in Chicago. "Never, never have I wanted so much to lead men and women to Christ as I do this time!"

There was a throbbing in his chest, and he had to hold to the organ to keep from falling, but Moody bravely preached the Gospel; and some fifty people responded to trust Christ. The next day, Moody left for home, and a month later he died. Up to the very end, Moody was "compelling them to come in."

5. The Multitudes: False Expectancy (14:25-35)

When Jesus left the Pharisee's house, great crowds followed Him, but He was not impressed by their enthusiasm. He knew that most of those in the crowd were not the least bit interested in spiritual things. Some wanted only to see miracles, others heard that He fed the hungry, and a few hoped He would overthrow Rome and establish David's promised kingdom. They were expecting the wrong things.

Jesus turned to the multitude and preached a sermon that deliberately thinned out the ranks. He made it clear that, when it comes to personal discipleship, He is more interested in *quality* than *quantity*. In the matter of saving lost souls, He wants His house to be filled (14:23); but in the matter of personal discipleship, He wants only those who are willing to pay the price.

A "disciple" is a learner, one who attaches himself or herself to a teacher in order to learn a trade or a subject. Perhaps our nearest modern equivalent is "apprentice," one who learns by watching and by doing. The word *disciple* was the most common name for the followers of Jesus Christ and is used 264 times in the Gospels and the Book of Acts.

Jesus seems to make a distinction between salvation and discipleship. Salvation is open to all who will come by faith, while discipleship is for believers willing to pay a price. Salvation means coming to the cross and trusting Jesus Christ, while discipleship means carrying the cross and following Jesus Christ. Jesus wants as many sinners saved as possible ("that My house may be filled"), but He cautions us not to take discipleship lightly; and in the three parables He gave, He made it clear that there is a price to pay.

To begin with, we must love Christ supremely, even more than we love our own flesh and blood (vv. 26-27). The word *hate* does not suggest positive antagonism but rather "to love less" (see Gen. 29:30-31; Mal. 1:2-3; and Matt. 10:37). Our love for Christ must be so strong that all other love is like hatred in comparison. In fact, we must hate our own lives and be willing to bear the cross after Him.

What does it mean to "carry the cross"? It means daily identification with Christ in shame, suffering, and surrender to God's will. It means death to self, to our own plans and ambitions, and a willingness to serve Him as He directs (John 12:23-28). A "cross" is something we willingly accept from God as part of His will for our lives. The Christian who called his noisy neighbors the "cross" he had to bear certainly did not understand the meaning of dying to self.

Jesus gave three parables to explain why He makes such costly demands on His followers: the man building a tower, the king fighting a war, and the salt losing its flavor. The usual interpretation is that believers are represented by the man building the tower and the king fighting the war, and we had better "count the cost" before we start, lest we start and not be able to finish. But I agree with Campbell Morgan that the builder and the king represent not the believer but Jesus Christ. *He is the One who must "count the cost" to see whether we are the kind of material He can use to build the church and battle the enemy.* He cannot get the job done with half-hearted followers who will not pay the price.

As I write this chapter, I can look up and see on my library shelves hundreds of volumes of Christian biographies and autobiographies, the stories of godly men and women who made great contributions to the building of the church and the battle against the enemy. They were willing to pay the price, and God blessed them and used them. They were people with "salt" in their character.

Jesus had already told His disciples that they were "the salt of the earth" (Matt. 5:13). When the sinner trusts Jesus Christ as Saviour, a miracle takes place and "clay" is turned into "salt." Salt was a valued item in that day; in fact, part of a soldier's pay was given in salt. (The words *salt* and *salary* are related; hence, the saying, "He's not worth his salt.")

Salt is a preservative, and God's people in this world are helping to retard the growth of evil and decay. Salt is also a purifying agent, an antiseptic that makes things cleaner. It may sting when it touches the wound, but it helps to kill infection. Salt gives flavor to things and, most of all, makes people thirsty. By our character and conduct, we ought to make others thirsty for the Lord Jesus Christ and the salvation that He alone can give.

Our modern salt is pure and does not lose its flavor, but the salt in Jesus' day was impure and could lose its flavor, especially if it came in contact with earth. Once the saltiness was gone, there was no way to restore it, and the salt was thrown out into the street to be walked on. When a disciple loses his Christian character, he is "good for nothing" and will eventually be "walked on" by others and bring disgrace to Christ.

Discipleship is serious business. If we are not true disciples, then Jesus cannot build the tower and fight the war. "There is always an *if* in connection with discipleship," wrote Oswald Chambers, "and it implies that we need not [be disciples] unless we like. There is never any compulsion; Jesus does not coerce us. There is only one way of being a disciple, and that is by being devoted to Jesus."

If we tell Jesus that we want to take up our cross and follow Him as His disciples, then He wants us to know exactly what we are getting into. He wants no false expectancy, no illusions, no bargains. He wants to use us as stones for building His church, soldiers for battling His enemies, and salt for bettering His world; *and He is looking for quality.*

After all, He was on His way to Jerusalem when He spoke these words, and look what happened to Him there! He does not ask us to do anything for Him that He has not already done for us.

To some, Jesus says, "You cannot be My disciples!" Why? Because they will not forsake all for Him, bear shame and reproach for Him, and let their love for Him control them.

And they are the losers.

Will *you* be His disciple?

2

The Joys of Salvation

Luke 15

When D. L. Moody was directing his Sunday School in Chicago, one boy walked several miles to attend; and somebody asked him, "Why don't you go to a Sunday School closer to home?"

His reply might have been used by the publicans and sinners in Jesus' day: "Because they love a feller over there."

It is significant that Jesus *attracted* sinners while the Pharisees *repelled* them. (What does this say about some of our churches today?) Lost sinners came to Jesus, not because He catered to them or compromised His message, but because He cared for them. He understood their needs and tried to help them, while the Pharisees criticized them and kept their distance (see 18:9-14). The Pharisees had a knowledge of the Old Testament Law and a desire for personal purity, yet they had no love for lost souls.

Three words summarize the message of this chapter: *lost, found,* and *rejoice.* Jesus spoke these parables to answer the accusations of the Pharisees and scribes who were scandalized at His behavior. It was bad enough that Jesus *welcomed* these outcasts and taught them, but He went so far as to *eat with them!* The Jewish religious leaders did not yet understand that the Son of man had "come to seek and to save that which was lost" (19:10). Even more, they were still blind to the fact that *they themselves were among the lost.*

This chapter makes it clear that there is one message of salvation: God welcomes and forgives repentant sinners. But these parables also reveal that there are *two aspects to this salvation.* There is *God's* part: the shepherd seeks the lost sheep, and the woman searches for the lost coin. But there is also *man's* part in salvation, for the wayward son willingly repented and returned home. To emphasize but one aspect is to give a false view of salvation, for both the sovereignty of God and the responsibility of man must be considered (see John 6:37; 2 Thes. 2:13-14).

Since one of the major themes of this chapter is joy, let's consider the three different joys that are involved in salvation. C. S. Lewis wrote, "Joy is the serious business of heaven," and it is a joy in which you and I can share.

1. The Joy of Finding (15:1-10)

The story about the lost sheep would touch the hearts of the men and boys in the crowd, and the women and girls would appreciate the story about the coin that was lost from the wedding necklace. Jesus sought to reach everybody's heart.

The lost sheep (vv. 3-7). The sheep was lost because of foolishness. Sheep have a tendency to go astray, and that is why they need a shepherd (Isa. 53:6; 1 Peter 2:25). The scribes and Pharisees had no problem seeing the publicans and sinners as "lost sheep," but they would not apply that image to themselves! And yet the prophet made it clear that all of us have sinned and gone astray, and that includes religious people.

The shepherd was responsible for each sheep; if one was

missing, the shepherd had to pay for it unless he could prove that it was killed by a predator (see Gen. 31:38-39; Ex. 22:10-13; Amos 3:12). This explains why he would leave the flock with the other shepherds, go and search for the missing animal, and then rejoice when he found it. Not to find the lost sheep meant money out of his own pocket, plus the disgrace of being known as a careless shepherd.

By leaving the ninety-nine sheep, the shepherd was not saying they were unimportant to him. They were safe but the lost sheep was in danger. The fact that the shepherd would go after *one* sheep is proof that each animal was dear to him. Jesus was not suggesting that the scribes and Pharisees were not in need of salvation, for they certainly were. We must not make every part of the parable mean something, otherwise we will turn it into an allegory and distort the message.

There is a fourfold joy expressed when a lost sinner comes to the Saviour. Although nothing is said in the story about how the sheep felt, there is certainly joy in the heart of the *person found*. Both Scripture (Acts 3:8; 8:39) and our own personal experience verify the joy of salvation.

But there is also the joy of the person who does the finding. Whenever you assist in leading a lost soul to faith in Christ, you experience a wonderful joy within. Others join with us in rejoicing as we share the good news of a new child of God in the family, and there is also joy in heaven (vv. 7, 10). The angels know better than we do what we are saved *from* and *to*, and they rejoice with us.

The lost coin (vv. 8-10). The sheep was lost because of its own native foolishness, but the coin was lost because of the carelessness of another. It is a sobering thought that our carelessness *at home* could result in a soul being lost.

When a Jewish girl married, she began to wear a headband of ten silver coins to signify that she was now a wife. It was the Jewish version of our modern wedding ring, and it would be considered a calamity for her to lose one of those coins. Palestinian houses were dark, so she had to light a lamp and search until she found the lost coin; and we can imagine her joy at finding it.

We must not press parabolic images too far, but it is worth noting that the coin would have on it the image of the ruler (20:19-25). The lost sinner bears the image of God, even though that image has been marred by sin. When a lost sinner is "found," God begins to restore that divine image through the power of the Spirit; and one day, the believer will be like Jesus Christ (Rom. 8:29; 2 Cor. 3:18; Col. 3:10; 1 John 3:1-2).

These two parables help us understand something of what it means to be lost. To begin with, it means being *out of place.* Sheep belong with the flock, coins belong on the chain, and lost sinners belong in fellowship with God. But to be lost also means *being out of service.* A lost sheep is of no value to the shepherd, a lost coin has no value to the owner, and a lost sinner cannot experience the enriching fulfillment God has for him in Jesus Christ.

But to turn this around, to be "found" (saved) means that you are back in place (reconciled to God), back in service (life has a purpose), and out of danger. No wonder the shepherd and the woman rejoiced and invited their friends to rejoice with them!

It is easy for us today to read these two parables and take their message for granted, but the people who first heard them must have been shocked. *Jesus was saying that God actually searches for lost sinners!* No wonder the scribes and Pharisees were offended, for there was no place in their legalistic theology for a God like that. They had forgotten that God had sought out Adam and Eve when they had sinned and hidden from God (Gen. 3:8-9). In spite of their supposed knowledge of Scripture, the scribes and Pharisees forgot that

God was like a father who pitied his wayward children (Ps. 103:8-14).

There are few joys that match the joy of finding the lost and bringing them to the Saviour. "The church has nothing to do but to save souls," said John Wesley, the founder of Methodism. "Therefore, spend and be spent in this work."

2. The Joy of Returning (15:11-24)

We call this story "The Parable of the Prodigal Son" (the word *prodigal* means "wasteful"), but it could also be called "The Parable of the Loving Father," for it emphasizes the graciousness of the father more than the sinfulness of the son. Unlike the shepherd and the woman in the previous parables, the father did not go out to seek the son, but it was the memory of his father's goodness that brought the boy to repentance and forgiveness (see Rom. 2:4). Note in the story the three experiences of the younger son.

Rebellion—he went to the far country (vv. 11-16). According to Jewish law, an elder son received twice as much as the other sons (Deut. 21:17), and a father could distribute his wealth during his lifetime if he wished. It was perfectly legal for the younger son to ask for his share of the estate and even to sell it, but it was certainly not a very loving thing on his part. It was as though he were saying to his father, "I wish you were dead!" Thomas Huxley said, "A man's worst difficulties begin when he is able to do just as he likes." How true!

We are always heading for trouble whenever we value things more than people, pleasure more than duty, and distant scenes more than the blessings we have right at home. Jesus once warned two disputing brothers, "Take heed and beware of covetousness!" (12:15) Why? Because the covetous person can never be satisfied, no matter how much he acquires, and a dissatisfied heart leads to a disappointed life. The prodigal learned the hard way that you cannot enjoy the things money can buy if you ignore the things money cannot buy.

"The far country" is not necessarily a distant place to which we must travel, because "the far country" exists first of all *in our hearts*. The younger son dreamed of "enjoying" his freedom far from home and away from his father and older brother. If the sheep was lost through foolishness and the coin through carelessness, then the son was lost because of willfulness. He wanted to have his own way so he rebelled against his own father and broke his father's heart.

But life in the far country was not what he expected. His resources ran out, his friends left him, a famine came, and the boy was forced to do for a stranger what he would not do for his own father—go to work! This scene in the drama is our Lord's way of emphasizing what sin really does in the lives of those who reject the Father's will. Sin promises freedom, but it only brings slavery (John 8:34); it promises success, but brings failure; it promises life, but "the wages of sin is death" (Rom. 6:23). The boy thought he would "find himself," but he only lost himself! When God is left out of our lives, enjoyment becomes enslavement.

Repentance—he came to himself (vv. 17-19). To "repent" means "to change one's mind," and that is exactly what the young man did as he cared for the pigs. (What a job for a Jewish boy!) He "came to himself," which suggests that up to this point he had not really "been himself." There is an "insanity" in sin that seems to paralyze the image of God within us and liberate the "animal" inside. Students of Shakespeare like to contrast two quotations that describe this contradiction in man's nature.

"What a piece of work is a man! How noble in reason! how infinite in faculty! in form, in moving, how express and admirable! in action how like an

angel! in apprehension how like a god!"
(*Hamlet,* II, ii)

"When he is best, he is a little worse than a
man; and when he is worst, he is little better than
a beast."
(*The Merchant of Venice,* I, ii)

The young man changed his mind about himself and his
situation, and he admitted that he was a sinner. He confessed
that his father was a generous man and that service at home
was far better than "freedom" in the far country. It is God's
goodness, not just man's badness, that leads us to repentance
(Rom. 2:4). If the boy had thought only about himself—his
hunger, his homesickness, his loneliness—he would have de-
spaired. But his painful circumstances helped him to see his
father in a new way, and this brought him hope. If his father
was so good to *servants,* maybe he would be willing to forgive a *son.*

Had he stopped there, the boy would have experienced only
regret or remorse (2 Cor. 7:10), but true repentance involves
the will as well as the mind and the emotions—"I will
arise . . . I will go . . . I will say. . . ." Our resolutions may be
noble, but unless we act upon them, they can never of themselves bring about any permanent good. If repentance is truly
the work of God (Acts 11:18), then the sinner will obey God
and put saving faith in Jesus Christ (Acts 20:21).

Rejoicing—he came to the father (vv. 20-24). Here Jesus
answered the accusations of the scribes and Pharisees (v. 2),
for the father not only ran to welcome his son, but he honored
the boy's homecoming by preparing a great feast and inviting
the village to attend. The father never did permit the younger
son to finish his confession; he interrupted him, forgave him,
and ordered the celebration to begin!

Of course, the father pictures to us the attitude of our Heavenly Father toward sinners who repent: He is rich in His mercy and grace, and great in His love toward them (Eph. 2:1-10). All of this is possible because of the sacrifice of His Son on the cross. No matter what some preachers (and singers) claim, we are not saved by God's love; God loves the whole world, and the whole world is not saved. We are saved by God's grace, and grace is *love that pays a price*.

In the East, old men do not run; yet the father ran to meet his son. Why? One obvious reason was his love for him and his desire to show that love. But there is something else involved. This wayward son had brought disgrace to his family and village and, according to Deuteronomy 21:18-21, he should have been stoned to death. *If the neighbors had started to stone him, they would have hit the father who was embracing him!* What a picture of what Jesus did for us on the cross!

Everything the younger son had hoped to find in the far country, he discovered back home: clothes, jewelry, friends, joyful celebration, love, and assurance for the future. What made the difference? Instead of saying, "Father, *give* me!" he said, "Father, *make* me!" He was willing to be a servant! Of course, the father did not ask him to "earn" his forgiveness, because no amount of good works can save us from our sins (Eph. 2:8-10; Titus 3:3-7). In the far country, the prodigal learned the meaning of misery; but back home, he discovered the meaning of mercy.

The ring was a sign of sonship, and the "best robe" (no doubt the father's) was proof of his acceptance back into the family (see Gen. 41:42; Isa. 61:10; 2 Cor. 5:21). Servants did not wear rings, shoes, or expensive garments. The feast was the father's way of showing his joy and sharing it with others. Had the boy been dealt with according to the Law, there would have been a funeral, not a feast. What a beautiful illustration of Psalm 103:10-14!

It is interesting to consider the father's description of his son's experience: he was dead, and is now alive; he was lost, and now is found. This is the spiritual experience of every lost sinner who comes to the Father through faith in Jesus Christ (Eph. 2:1-10; John 5:24). Note the parallels between the prodigal's coming to the father and our coming to the Father through Christ (John 14:6):

The Prodigal	*Jesus Christ*
He was lost (v. 24)	"I am the way"
He was ignorant (v. 17)	"I am the truth"
He was dead (v. 24)	"I am the life"

There is only one way to come to the Father, and that is through faith in Jesus Christ. Have you come home?

3. The Joy of Forgiving (15:25-32)

At this point in the parable, the scribes and Pharisees felt confident that they had escaped our Lord's judgment, for He had centered His attention on the publicans and sinners, pictured by the prodigal son. But Jesus continued the story and introduced the elder brother, who is a clear illustration of the scribes and Pharisees. The publicans and sinners were guilty of the obvious sins of the flesh, but the Pharisees and scribes were guilty of sins of the spirit (2 Cor. 7:1). Their outward actions may have been blameless, but their inward attitudes were abominable (see Matt. 23:25-28).

We must admit that the elder brother had some virtues that are commendable. He worked hard and always obeyed his father. He never brought disgrace either to the home or to the village, and apparently he had enough friends so that he could have planned an enjoyable party (v. 29). He seems like a good solid citizen and, compared to his younger brother, almost a saint.

However, important as obedience and diligence are, they are not the only tests of character. Jesus taught that the two greatest commandments are to love God and to love others (10:25-28), but the elder brother broke both of these divine commandments. He did not love God (represented in the story by the father), and he did not love his brother. The elder brother would not forgive his brother who wasted the family inheritance and disgraced the family name. But neither would he forgive his father who had graciously forgiven the young man those very sins!

When you examine the sins of the elder brother, you can easily understand why he pictures the scribes and Pharisees. To begin with, he was *self-righteous*. He openly announced the sins of his brother, but he could not see his own sins (see 18:9-14). The Pharisees defined sin primarily in terms of outward actions, not inward attitudes. They completely missed the message of the Sermon on the Mount and its emphasis on inward attitudes and holiness of heart (Matt. 5–7).

Pride was another one of his failings. Just think, he had served his father all those years and had *never* disobeyed his will! What a testimony! But his heart was not in his work, and he was always dreaming of throwing a big party at which he and his friends could enjoy themselves. He was only a drudge. Like the Prophet Jonah, the elder brother did God's will *but not from the heart* (Eph. 6:6; Jonah 4). He was a hard worker and a faithful worker—qualities to be commended—but his work was not a "labor of love" that would please his father.

You cannot help but notice his *unconcern for his missing brother.* Imagine having to be told that his brother had come home! The father watched for the younger son day after day and finally saw him afar off, but the elder brother did not know his brother was home until one of the servants told him.

Even though he knew it would make his father happy, the

elder brother did not want his younger brother to come home. Why should he share his estate with somebody who had wasted his own inheritance? Why should he even share the father's love with somebody who had brought shame to the family and the village? Reports of the prodigal's lifestyle only made the elder brother look good, and perhaps this would make the father love his obedient son even more. No doubt about it—the arrival of the younger son was a threat to the older son.

Perhaps the most disturbing thing about the elder son was his fierce *anger*. He was angry at both his father and his brother and would not go into the house and share in the joyful celebration.

Anger is a normal emotion and it need not be sinful. "Be ye angry, and sin not" (Eph. 4:26, quoting Ps. 4:4). Moses, David, the prophets, and our Lord Jesus displayed holy anger at sin, and so should we today. The Puritan preacher Thomas Fuller said that anger was one of the "sinews of the soul." Aristotle gave good advice when he wrote: "Anybody can become angry. That is easy. But to be angry with the right person and to the right degree and at the right time and for the right purpose and in the right way—that is not within everybody's power and is not easy."

The elder brother was angry with his father because his father had given the younger son the feast that the elder brother had always wanted. "You never gave me so much as a goat," he said to his father, "but you killed for him the valuable fatted calf!" The elder brother's dreams were all shattered because the father had forgiven the prodigal.

Of course the elder brother was angry at his younger brother for getting all that attention and receiving the father's special gifts. As far as the elder brother was concerned, *the younger brother deserved none of it*. Had he been faithful? No! Had he obeyed the father? No! Then why should he be treated with such kindness and love?

The Pharisees had a religion of good works. By their fasting, studying, praying, and giving, they hoped to earn blessings from God and merit eternal life. They knew little or nothing about the grace of God. However, it was not what they did, but what they did not do, that alienated them from God. (See Matt. 23:23-24.) When they saw Jesus receiving and forgiving irreligious people, they rebelled against it. Even more, they failed to see that *they themselves also needed the Saviour.*

The same father who ran to meet the prodigal came out of the house of feasting to plead with the older son. How gracious and condescending our Father is, and how patient He is with our weaknesses! The father explained that he would have been willing to host a feast for the older boy and his friends, but the boy had never asked him. Furthermore, ever since the division of the estate, the elder brother owned everything, and he could use it as he pleased.

The elder brother refused to go in; he stayed outside and pouted. He missed the joy of forgiving his brother and restoring the broken fellowship, the joy of pleasing his father and uniting the family again. How strange that the elder brother could speak peaceably to a servant boy, but he could not speak peaceably to his brother or father!

If we are out of fellowship with God, we cannot be in fellowship with our brothers and sisters and, conversely, if we harbor an unforgiving attitude toward others, we cannot be in communion with God (see 1 John 4:18-21; Matt. 5:21-26). When they show true repentance, we must forgive those who sin, and we should seek to restore them in grace and humility (Matt. 18:15-35; Gal. 6:1-5; Eph. 4:32).

The father had the last word, so we do not know how the story ended. (See Jonah 4 for a parallel narrative.) We do know that the scribes and Pharisees continued to oppose Jesus and separate themselves from His followers, and that their leaders eventually brought about our Lord's arrest and death. In spite of the Father's pleading, they would not come in.

Everybody in this chapter experienced joy except the elder brother. The shepherd, the woman, and their friends all experienced the joy of finding. The younger son experienced the joy of returning and being received by a loving, gracious father. The father experienced the joy of receiving his son back safe and sound. But the elder brother would not forgive his brother, so he had no joy. He could have repented and attended the feast, but he refused; so he stayed outside and suffered.

In my years of preaching and pastoral ministry, I have met elder brothers (and sisters!) who have preferred nursing their anger to enjoying the fellowship of God and God's people. Because they will not forgive, they have alienated themselves from the church and even from their family; they are sure that everyone else is wrong and they alone are right. They can talk loudly about the sins of others, but they are blind to their own sins.

"I never forgive!" General Oglethorpe said to John Wesley, to which Wesley replied, "Then, sir, I hope you never sin."

Don't stand outside! Come in and enjoy the feast!

3

The Right and Wrong of Riches

Luke 16

The *Wall Street Journal* quoted an anonymous wit who defined *money* as "an article which may be used as a universal passport to everywhere except heaven, and as a universal provider for everything except happiness." The writer might have added that money is also a provoker of covetousness and competition, a wonderful servant but a terrible master. The love of money is still "a root of all kinds of evil" (1 Tim. 6:10, NKJV) and has helped fill our world with corruption and lust (1 Peter 1:4).

When you read our Lord's sermons and parables, you are struck with the fact that He had a great deal to say about material wealth. He ministered to people who, for the most part, were poor and who thought that acquiring more wealth was the solution to all their problems. Jesus was not blind to the needs of the poor, and by His example and teaching, He encouraged His followers to share what they had with others. The early church was a fellowship of people who willingly shared their possessions with the less fortunate (Acts 2:44-47; 4:33-37).

In His portrait of the prodigal and the elder brother, Jesus described two opposite philosophies of life. Prior to his repentance, the prodigal *wasted* his life, but his elder brother only *spent* his life as a faithful drudge. Both attitudes are wrong, for the Christian approach to life is that we should *invest* our lives for the good of others and the glory of God. This chapter emphasizes that truth: life is a stewardship, and we must use our God-given opportunities faithfully. One day we must give an account to the Lord of what we have done with all He has given to us, so we had better heed what Jesus says in this chapter about the right and wrong use of wealth.

Neither of the two accounts in this chapter is called a parable either by Jesus or by Luke, so it is likely that our Lord was describing actual happenings. However, whether they are actual events or only parables, the spiritual values are the same.

1. The Right Use of Wealth (16:1-13)

A *foolish steward* (vv. 1-2). A steward is someone who manages another's wealth. He does not own that wealth himself, but he has the privilege of enjoying it and using it for the profit of his master. The most important thing about a steward is that he serve his master faithfully (1 Cor. 4:2). When he looks at the riches around him, the steward must remember that they belong to his master, not to him personally, and that they must be used in a way that will please and profit the master.

This particular steward *forgot* that he was a steward and began to act as if he were the owner. He became a "prodigal steward" who wasted his master's wealth. His master heard about it and immediately asked for an inventory of his goods and an audit of his books. He also fired his steward.

Before we judge this man too severely, let's examine our own lives to see how faithful we have been as stewards of what God has given to us. To begin with, we are stewards of the *material wealth* that we have, whether much or little; and we will one day have to answer to God for the way we have acquired it and used it.

Christian stewardship goes beyond paying God a tithe of our income and then using the remainder as we please. True stewardship means that we thank God for *all* that we have (Deut. 8:11-18) and use it as He directs. Giving God 10 percent of our income is a good way to begin our faithful stewardship, but we must remember that God should control what we do with the remaining 90 percent as well.

We are also stewards of *our time* (Eph. 5:15-17). The phrase "redeeming the time" comes from the business world and means "buying up the opportunity." Time is eternity, minted into precious minutes and handed to us to use either wisely or carelessly. The main lesson of this narrative is that the steward, as dishonest as he was, used his opportunity wisely and prepared for the future. Life ceased to be "enjoyment" and became "investment."

Christians are stewards of the *gifts and abilities* God has given them (1 Peter 4:10), and we must use those gifts and abilities to serve others. The thief says, "What's yours is mine—I'll take it!" The selfish man says, "What's mine is mine—I'll keep it!" But the Christian must say, "What's mine is a gift from God—I'll share it!" We are stewards and we must use our abilities to win the lost, encourage the saints, and meet the needs of hurting people.

Finally, God's people are stewards of the Gospel (1 Thes. 2:4). God has committed the treasure of His truth to us (2 Cor. 4:7), and we must guard this treasure (1 Tim. 6:20) and invest it in the lives of others (2 Tim. 2:2). The enemy wants to rob the church of this treasure (Jude 3-4), and we must be alert and courageous.

Like this steward, we will one day have to give an account of our stewardship (Rom. 14:10-12; 2 Cor. 5:10ff). If we have been faithful, the Lord will give us His commendation and reward (Matt. 25:21; 1 Cor. 4:5); but if we have not been faithful, we will lose those blessings, even though we will be saved and enter heaven (1 Cor. 3:13-15).

Vance Havner often said, "God called us to play the game, not keep the score." If we are faithful stewards, God will reward us generously, and that reward will bring glory to His name.

A wise steward (vv. 3-8). The steward knew he would lose his job. He could not change the past, but he could prepare for the future. How? By making friends of his master's creditors so that they would take him in when his master threw him out. He gave each of them a generous discount, provided they paid up immediately, and they were only too glad to cooperate. Even his master complimented him on his clever plan (v. 8).

Jesus did not commend the steward for robbing his master or for encouraging others to be dishonest. *Jesus commended the man for his wise use of opportunity.* "The children of this world" are experts at seizing opportunities for making money and friends and getting ahead. God's people should take heed and be just as wise when it comes to managing the spiritual affairs of life. "The children of this world" are wiser only "in their generation"; they see the things of time, but not the things of eternity. Because the child of God lives "with eternity's values in view," he should be able to make far better use of his opportunities.

The application (vv. 9-13). Jesus gave three admonitions, based on the experience of the steward.

First, He admonishes us to *use our opportunities wisely* (v. 9). One of these days, life will end, and we will not be able to earn or use money. Therefore, while we have the opportunity, we must invest our money in "making friends" for the Lord. This means winning people to Christ who will one day welcome us to heaven. Our lives and our resources will one day end, so it behooves us to use them wisely.

It is tragic to see how God's wealth is being wasted by Christians who live as though Jesus never died and judgment is never coming. The old couplet is certainly true:

> The only difference between men and boys
> Is that men buy more expensive toys.

The heritage of the past must be used wisely in the present to guarantee spiritual dividends in the future. All of us should want to meet people in heaven who trusted Christ because we helped to pay the bill for Gospel witness around the world, starting at home. Thoreau wrote that a man is wealthy in proportion to the number of things he can afford to do without, and he was right. I once heard the late Jacob Stam pray, "Lord, the only thing we know about sacrifice is how to spell the word." I wonder if today some of us can even spell the word!

Our Lord's second admonition is *be faithful in the way you use your material wealth* (vv. 10-12). He makes it clear that you cannot divorce the "spiritual" from the "material." Notice the contrasts:

The material	*The spiritual*
The god "Mammon"	The true God
that which is least	that which is much
false riches	true riches
that which is another's	that which is yours

Why is our Lord so concerned about the way we use money? Because money is not neutral; it is basically evil ("the mammon of unrighteousness"), and only God can sanctify it and use it for good. It is significant that both Paul and Peter called money "filthy lucre" (1 Tim. 3:3, 8; Titus 1:7, 11; 1 Peter 5:2). Apparently by its very nature, money defiles and debases those who love it and let it control their lives. "We cannot safely use mammon," writes Richard Foster, "until we are absolutely clear that we are dealing, not just with mammon, but with unrighteous mammon" (*Money, Sex and Power*, Harper & Row, p. 57).

People who are unfaithful in the way they use money are also unfaithful in the way they use the "true riches" of the kingdom of God. We cannot be orthodox in our theology and at the same time heretical in the way we use money. God will not commit His true riches to individuals or ministries that waste money and will not give an honest accounting to the people who have supported them. When it came to money, Paul was very careful that everything was honest "not only in the sight of the Lord, but also in the sight of men" (2 Cor. 8:21).

Finally, the Lord admonishes us to *be wholly devoted to God and single-minded* (v. 13; and see Matt. 6:19-24). We cannot love or serve two masters, anymore than we can walk in two directions at one time. If we choose to serve money, then we cannot serve God. If we choose to serve God, then we will not serve money. Jesus is demanding *integrity*, total devotion to God that puts Him first in everything (Matt. 6:33).

If God is our master, then money will be our servant, and we will use our resources in the will of God. But if God is not our master, then *we will become the servants of money*, and money is a terrible master! We will start *wasting* our lives instead of *investing* them, and we will one day find ourselves "friendless" as we enter the gates of glory.

Henry Fielding wrote, "Make money your god and it will plague you like the devil!" Jesus said, "Make money your servant and use today's opportunities as investments in tomorrow's dividends." Be a wise steward! There are souls to win to the Saviour, and our money can help get the job done.

2. The Wrong Use of Money (16:14-31)

Jesus had been speaking primarily to His disciples, but the Pharisees had been listening, and their response was anything but spiritual. They sneered at Him! (The Greek word means "to turn up one's nose.") In spite of their strict religious practices, they loved money and cultivated values that were godless. They professed to trust God, but they measured life by wealth and possessions, the same as the unbelieving worldly crowd. *Far too many professed Christians today are making the same mistake.* With their lips, they honor the Lord; but with their wealth, they live like the world.

The Pharisees needed to stop "drifting" with the crowd and start "pressing into the kingdom" as many others were doing. The Pharisees had rejected the ministry of John the Baptist and permitted him to be killed, even though they knew he was God's prophet. They were also rejecting the ministry of Jesus Christ and would ultimately ask Pilate to have Him crucified. When your life is controlled by the love of money, you open the door to every kind of sin.

The Law and the Prophets were "until John," for John introduced the Saviour to the nation and announced the arrival of the kingdom. But that did not mean that the Law was discredited or destroyed, for in Jesus Christ, the Law has been fulfilled (Matt. 5:17-20). The Pharisees prided themselves in their faithful obedience to the Law of Moses, but they did not receive the Saviour of whom Moses wrote!

Why did Jesus talk about divorce and remarriage when His basic discussion was about covetousness? The scribes and Pharisees were divided on this question, and perhaps they wanted to provoke Jesus into an argument, but He thwarted their plans. (In most marriages and divorces, money is involved, so the topic was not completely foreign to the discussion.) Some of the Jews were very lax in their views of divorce and remarriage, while others were very strict. Jesus had spoken about this subject before, so it was not a new teaching (Matt. 5:31-32).

Having silenced the sneering Pharisees, Jesus then gave them a vivid description of what would happen to them if they continued in their covetousness and unbelief. The account focuses on an anonymous rich man and a beggar named Lazarus ("God is my help"), and it warns us against covetousness by presenting several contrasts.

A contrast in life (vv. 19-21). This man was indeed rich if he could afford daily to wear expensive clothes and host splendid feasts. The one word that best describes his lifestyle is "flamboyant." He was definitely among "the rich and famous," and other people admired and envied him.

Why is one man wealthy and another man poor? Had the Jewish people obeyed God's commandments concerning the Sabbatical Year and the Year of Jubilee, there would have been little or no poverty in the land, for the wealth and real estate could not have fallen into the hands of a few wealthy people (see Lev. 25, and note Ex. 23:11; Deut. 14:28-29). The Old Testament prophets denounced the rich for amassing great estates and exploiting the widows and the poor (Isa. 3:15; 10:2; Amos 2:6; 4:1; 5:11-12; 8:4-6; Hab. 2:9-13). In Jesus' day, Palestine was under the rule of Rome, and life was very difficult for the common people.

Lazarus was sick and possibly crippled, because he was "laid" at the rich man's gate daily (see Acts 3:1-2). The only attention he got was from the dogs! The rich man could easily have assisted Lazarus, but he ignored him and went on enjoying his recognition and his riches. Life was comfortable for him and he felt secure.

The rich man obviously had no concept of stewardship, or he would have used part of his wealth to help Lazarus. It is a mystery why he even allowed the beggar to camp at his front door. Perhaps he thought that providing a place for the man was ministry enough, and it may be that some of his wealthy guests occasionally gave Lazarus alms. Did any of them ever recall what the Old Testament had to say about the care of the poor, such as Proverbs 14:21; 19:17; 21:13; or 28:27?

A contrast in death (v. 22). "The rich and poor meet together; the Lord is the Maker of them all" (Prov. 22:2). As John Donne said, death is the "great leveler." The rich man died in spite of his wealth (Ps. 49:6-9) and "was buried," no doubt with an expensive funeral. But when Lazarus died, he was carried to Abraham's bosom. What a difference! Perhaps the beggar's body did not even have a decent burial, although the Jews were usually compassionate in such cases. Lazarus certainly did not have the traditional Jewish funeral, with its paid mourners, costly spices, and elaborate tomb. After Lazarus's body was taken away, the neighbors probably said, "Well, we're glad he's not around anymore!"

Death takes place when the spirit leaves the body (James 2:26). But death is not the end; it is the beginning of a whole new existence in another world. For the Christian, death means to be present with the Lord (2 Cor. 5:1-8; Phil. 1:21). For the unbeliever, death means to be away from God's presence and in torment.

A contrast in eternity (vv. 23-31). The *King James Version* uses the word *hell* in verse 23, but the Greek word is not "hell" but "hades." It is the temporary realm of the dead as they await the judgment. The permanent place of punishment for the lost is "hell," the lake of fire. One day, death will give up the bodies and hades will give up the souls (Rev. 20:13, where "hell" should be "hades"), and the lost will stand before Christ in judgment (Rev. 20:10-15).

From our Lord's description, we learn that hades had two sections: a paradise portion called "Abraham's bosom," and a punishment portion. It is believed by many theologians that our Lord emptied the paradise part of hades when He arose from the dead and returned to the Father (John 20:17; Eph. 4:8-10). We know that today "paradise" is in heaven, where Jesus reigns in glory (23:43; 2 Cor. 12:1-4). There is no indication in Scripture that souls in heaven or in hades can communicate with each other or with people on earth.

This narrative refutes so-called "soul sleep," for both the rich man and Lazarus were conscious, one enjoying comfort and the other suffering torment. It is a solemn thing to ponder one's eternal destiny and realize the reality of divine punishment.

C. S. Lewis was told about a gravestone inscription that read: "Here lies an atheist—all dressed up and no place to go." Lewis quietly replied, "I bet he wishes that were so!"

The interesting thing is that, in hades, the rich man began to pray! First, he prayed for himself, that Abraham would have mercy on him and allow Lazarus to bring him some comfort (vv. 23-26). Even a drop of cool water would be welcomed. What a change from his sumptuous feasts when slaves ran to do his bidding!

The word *torment* is used four times in this account, and it speaks of definite pain. This is the same word that is used for the doom feared by the evil spirits (Mark 5:7) and the judgments God will send on an unrepentant world (Rev. 9:5; 11:10; 20:10). If hell is the permanent prison of the damned, then hades is the temporary jail, and the suffering in both is very real.

People ask, "How can a loving God even permit such a place as hell to exist, let alone send people there?" But in asking that question, they reveal that they do not understand either the love of God or the wickedness of sin. God's love is a *holy* love ("God is light," 1 John 1:5), not a shallow sentiment, and sin is rebellion against a holy and loving God. God does not "send people to hell." They send themselves there by refusing to heed His call and believe on His Son. The "unbelieving" are named second on the list of the people who go to hell, even before the murderers and the liars (Rev. 21:8; also see John 3:18-21, 36).

Abraham gave two reasons why Lazarus could not bring the comfort that was requested: the character of the rich man and the character of the eternal state. The rich man had lived for the "good things" of earth, and had experienced abundant temporal blessings. He had his reward (Matt. 6:2, 5, 16). He had determined his own destiny by leaving God out of his life, and now neither his character nor his destiny could be changed. Lazarus could not leave his place of comfort and make even a brief visit to the place of torment.

Then the rich man prayed for his brothers (vv. 27-31). He did not say, "I'm glad my brothers will also come here. We'll have a wonderful time together!" Occasionally you hear a lost person say, "Well, I don't mind if I go to hell. I'll have a lot of company!" *But there is no friendship or "company" in hell!* Hell is place of torment and loneliness. It is not an eternal New Year's Eve party at which sinners have a good time doing what they used to do on earth.

Verse 28 suggests that Lazarus had testified to the rich man and probably to his brothers, but none of them had taken his witness seriously. But now, Lazarus' testimony is very important! The brothers knew that Lazarus had died, so if the beggar appeared to them, they would be frightened and would listen to his witness. *People in hades have a concern for the lost, but they cannot do anything about it.*

Abraham explained that only one thing could prevent the five men from eventually joining their brother: they needed to hear the Word of God and respond to it by faith. Moses and the prophets tell sinners how to repent and be saved, and the Jews heard them read every Sabbath in the synagogue.

Though miracles can attest to the authority of the preacher, they cannot produce either conviction or conversion in the hearts of the lost. Faith that is based solely on miracles is not saving faith (John 2:23-25). A man named Lazarus *did* come back from the dead, *and some of the people wanted to kill him!* (See John 11:43-57; 12:10.) Those who claim that there can be no effective evangelism without "signs and wonders" need to ponder this passage and also John 10:41-42.

In the rich man's lifetime, God had spoken to him in many ways. God had permitted him to have riches, yet he did not repent (Rom. 2:4-5). Lazarus had witnessed to the rich man, and so had the Old Testament Scriptures that were familiar to the Jews, but his heart remained unbelieving. The fact that Lazarus died first was a strong witness to the rich man, a reminder that one day he would also die, but even a death at his very doorstep did not melt the man's heart.

In spite of the fact that he was in torment in hades, the rich man did not change; he was still self-centered. He prayed, but it was for *his* comfort and the safety of *his* family. He was not concerned about other lost sinners; his only concern was his five brothers. He argued with God instead of submitting to His will. This indicates that the punishment of lost sinners is not remedial; it does not improve them. Hades and hell are not hospitals for the sick; they are prisons for the condemned.

Dr. Luke does not tell us how the covetous Pharisees responded to this account. They certainly knew Moses and the prophets, and this meant even greater responsibility—*and greater condemnation* (John 12:35-41).

We must remind ourselves that the rich man was not condemned because he was rich, nor was Lazarus saved because he was poor. Abraham was a very wealthy man, yet he was not in torment in hades. The rich man trusted in his riches and did not trust in the Lord.

"The safest road to hell," wrote C. S. Lewis, "is the gradual

one—the gentle slope, soft underfoot, without sudden turn-
ings, without milestones, without signposts."

"For what shall it profit a man, if he shall gain the whole
world, and lose his own soul?" (Mark 8:36)

Jesus asked that question.

What is your answer?

4

Things That Really Matter

Luke 17

As Jesus made His way to Jerusalem, He continued to teach His disciples and prepare them for what He would suffer there. But He was also preparing them for the time when He would no longer be with them and they would be ministering to others in His place. It was a critical period in their lives.

In this chapter, Luke recorded lessons that Jesus gave His disciples about some of the essentials of the Christian life: forgiveness (vv. 1-6), faithfulness (vv. 7-10), thankfulness (vv. 11-19), and preparedness (vv. 20-37).

1. Forgiveness (17:1-6)

After Jesus warned the Pharisees about the sin of loving money (16:14-31), He then turned to His disciples to warn them about possible sins in their lives, for occasions to stumble ("offenses") are an unfortunate part of life. After all, we are all sinners living in a sinful world. But we must take heed not to cause others to stumble, for it is a serious thing to sin against a fellow believer and tempt him or her to sin (Rom. 14:13; 1 Cor. 10:32; 1 John 2:10).

By "these little ones" (v. 2), Jesus was referring not only to children but also to young believers who were learning how to follow the Lord (10:21 and Matt. 18:1-6). Since Luke 17:1-10 is part of a context that begins with 15:1, "little ones" would include the publicans and sinners who had come to believe in Jesus Christ. The Pharisees had criticized Jesus, and this might well have caused these new believers to stumble. So serious is this sin that a person would be better off cast alive into the sea, never to be seen again, than to deliberately cause others to stumble and sin.

But suppose *you* are not the one who does the sinning. Suppose another believer sins against you. Jesus anticipated this question in verses 3-4 and instructed us what to do. First, we must have a personal concern for each other and obey His warning, "Take heed to yourselves." This means that we should lovingly watch over each other and do all we can to keep one another from sinning.

If a brother or sister does sin against us, we should give a private loving rebuke. Our tendency might be to feel hurt down inside, nurse a grudge, and then tell others what happened to us, but this is the wrong approach (see Matt. 18:15-20). "Speaking the truth in love" (Eph. 4:15) is the first step toward solving personal differences.

Our aim is not to embarrass or hurt the offender, but to encourage him or her to repent (Gal. 6:1). If the offender does repent, then we must forgive (Eph. 4:32; and see Matt. 5:43-48). In fact, we must be *in the habit of forgiving*, for others might sin against us seven times a day—or even seventy times seven! (Matt. 18:21ff) No one is likely to commit that much sin in one day, but this use of hyperbole emphasized the point Jesus was making: do not enumerate the sins of others, for love "keeps no record of wrongs" (1 Cor. 13:4-6). We should always be ready to forgive others, for one day we may want them to forgive us!

We might have expected the disciples to respond with the prayer, "Increase our love!" Certainly love is a key element in forgiveness, but faith is even more important. *It takes living faith to obey these instructions and forgive others.* Our obedience in forgiving others shows that we are trusting God to take care of the consequences, handle the possible misunderstandings, and work everything out for our good and His glory.

Mature Christians understand that forgiveness is not a cheap exchange of words, the way squabbling children often flippantly say "I'm sorry" to each other. True forgiveness always involves pain; somebody has been hurt and there is a price to pay in healing the wound. Love *motivates* us to forgive, but faith *activates* that forgiveness so that God can use it to work blessings in the lives of His people.

Our Lord's image of the mustard seed conveys the idea of life and growth. The mustard seed is very small, but it has life in it and, therefore, it can grow and produce fruit (Mark 4:30-32). If our faith is a *living* faith (James 2:14-26), it will grow and enable us to obey God's commands. "Commit thy way unto the Lord; trust also in Him; and He shall bring it to pass" (Ps. 37:5). Forgiveness is a test of both our faith and our love.

Human nature being what it is, there will always be offenses that can easily become opportunities for sin. God's people must get into the habit of facing these offenses honestly and lovingly, and forgiving others when they repent. The Anglican pastor and poet George Herbert wrote, "He who cannot forgive breaks the bridge over which he himself must pass."

2. Faithfulness (17:7-10)

The introductory word *but* indicates that Jesus was now going to balance one lesson with another. There was a danger that the Twelve might get so carried away with transplanting trees that they would ignore the everyday responsibilities of life! Faith that does not result in faithfulness will not accomplish God's work. It is good to have faith to do the *difficult* (vv. 1-3) and the *impossible* (vv. 4-6), but it is essential that we have faith to do even the *routine tasks* our Master has committed to us. Privileges must always be balanced with responsibilities.

The servant in the story was evidently a "jack-of-all-trades," for he was responsible for farming, shepherding, and cooking. It was not unusual for people with only modest means to hire at least one servant, but Jesus described a situation which in that day was unthinkable: a master ministering to his servant! In fact, He introduced the story with a phrase that means, "Can any of you imagine . . . ?" Their answer had to be, "No, we cannot imagine such a thing!"

Jesus had already discussed His relationship to His servants *and had promised to serve them if they were faithful* (12:35-38). He Himself was among them as a servant (22:27), even though He was Master of all. This story emphasizes faithfulness to duty no matter what the demands might be, and the argument is from the lesser to the greater. If a common servant is faithful to obey the orders of his master who does not reward (thank) him, how much more ought Christ's disciples obey their loving Master, who has promised to reward them graciously!

A faithful servant should not expect any special reward, since he did only what he was told to do. The word translated "unprofitable" means "without need"—that is, "nobody owes us anything." The servant was indeed profitable; after all, he cared for his master's fields, flocks, and food. The statement means, "My master does not owe me anything extra." *The fact that Jesus will reward His servants is wholly a matter of God's grace.* We do not deserve anything because we have obeyed Him and served Him.

As His servants, we must beware lest we have the wrong attitude toward our duties. There are two extremes to avoid: merely doing our duty in a slavish way *because we have to,* or doing our duty *because we hope to gain a reward.* Christian industrialist R. G. LeTourneau used to say, "If you give because it pays, *it won't pay.*" This principle also applies to service. Both extremes are seen in the attitudes of the elder brother (15:25-32) who was miserably obedient, always hoping that his father would let him have a party with his friends.

What then is the proper attitude for Christian service? "Doing the will of God from the heart" (Eph. 6:6). "If you love Me, keep My commandments" (John 14:15, NKJV). To the person who is born again, "His commandments are not grievous" (1 John 5:3). Serving Him is a delight, not just a duty, and we obey Him because we love Him. "I delight to do Thy will, O my God: yea, Thy law is within my heart" (Ps. 40:8).

3. Thankfulness (17:11-19)

Between verses 10 and 11, the events of John 11 occurred as the Lord Jesus made His way to Jerusalem. At the border of Samaria and Judea, Jesus healed ten lepers at one time, and the fact that the miracle involved a Samaritan made it even more significant (see 10:30-37). Jesus used this event to teach a lesson about gratitude to God.

The account begins with *ten unclean men* (vv. 11-13), all of whom were lepers (see the comments on 5:12-15). The Jews and Samaritans would not normally live together, but misery loves company and all ten were outcasts. What difference does birth make if you are experiencing a living death? But these men had hope, for Jesus was there, and they cried out for mercy. The word translated "master" is the same one Peter used (5:5) and means "chief commander." They knew that Jesus was totally in command of even disease and death, and they trusted Him to help them.

The account continues by referring to *nine ungrateful men* (v. 17). Jesus commanded the men to go show themselves to the priest, which in itself was an act of faith, for they had not yet been cured. When they turned to obey, they were completely healed, for their obedience was evidence of their faith (see 2 Kings 5:1-14).

You would have expected all ten men to run to Jesus and thank Him for a new start in life, but only one did so—and he was not even a Jew. How grateful the men should have been for the providence of God that brought Jesus into their area, for the love that caused Him to pay attention to them and their need, and for the grace and power of God that brought about their healing. They should have formed an impromptu men's chorus and sung Psalm 103 together!

But before we judge them too harshly, what is our own "GQ"—"Gratitude Quotient"? How often do we take our blessings for granted and fail to thank the Lord? "Oh that men would praise the Lord for His goodness, and for His wonderful works to the children of men!" (Ps. 107:8, 15, 21, 31) Too often we are content to enjoy the gift but we forget the Giver. We are quick to pray but slow to praise.

The next time you sing "Now Thank We All Our God," try to remember that Martin Rinkhart wrote it during the Thirty Years' War when his pastoral duties were most difficult. He conducted as many as forty funerals a day, including that of his own wife; yet he wrote those beautiful words as a table grace for his family. In spite of war and plague around him and sorrow within him, he was able to give thanks to the Lord from a grateful heart.

Luke's account closes with *one unusual man* (vv. 15-19). The Samaritan shouted "Glory to God!" and fell at Jesus' feet to praise Him and give thanks. It would have been logical for him to have followed the other men and gone to the temple, but he first came to the Lord Jesus with his sacrifice of praise

(Heb. 13:15; Ps. 107:22). This pleased the Lord more than all the sacrifices the other men offered, even though they were obeying the Law (Ps. 51:15-17). Instead of *going to* the priest, the Samaritan *became* a priest, and he built his altar at the feet of Jesus (read Ps. 116:12-19).

By coming to Jesus, the man received something greater than physical healing: he was also saved from his sins. Jesus said, "Your faith has saved you" (literal translation), the same words He spoke to the repentant woman who anointed His feet (7:50). The Samaritan's nine friends were declared clean by the priest, but he was declared *saved* by the Son of God! While it is wonderful to experience the miracle of physical healing, it is even more wonderful to experience the miracle of eternal salvation.

Every child of God should cultivate the grace of gratitude. It not only opens the heart to further blessings but glorifies and pleases the Father. An unthankful heart is fertile soil for all kinds of sins (Rom. 1:21ff).

4. Preparedness (17:20-37)

The Jewish people lived in an excited atmosphere of expectancy, particularly at the Passover season when they commemorated their deliverance from Egypt. They longed for another Moses who would deliver them from their bondage. Some had hoped that John the Baptist would be the deliverer, and then the attention focused on Jesus (John 6:15). The fact that He was going to Jerusalem excited them all the more (19:11). Perhaps He would establish the promised kingdom!

The Pharisees were the custodians of the Law (Matt. 23:2-3), so they had the right to ask Jesus when He thought the kingdom of God would appear. It was customary for Jewish teachers to discuss these subjects publicly, and Jesus gave them a satisfactory answer. However, He reserved His detailed lessons for His disciples.

The word translated "observation" (v. 20) is used only here in the New Testament and means in classical Greek "to observe the future by signs." It carries the idea of spying, lying in wait, and even scientific investigation. The point Jesus made was that God's kingdom would not come with great "outward show" so that people could predict its arrival and plot its progress.

The Pharisees' question was legitimate, but it was also tragic; for Jesus had been ministering among them for some three years, and these men were still in spiritual darkness. They did not understand who Jesus was or what He was seeking to accomplish. Their views of the kingdom were political, not spiritual; Jewish, not universal. Jesus did not deny that there would be a future earthly kingdom, but He did emphasize the importance of the *spiritual* kingdom that could be entered only by the new birth (John 3:1-8).

The statement "the kingdom of God is within you" has challenged Bible translators and interpreters for centuries, and many explanations have been given. One thing we can be sure of is that He was not telling the unbelieving Pharisees that they had the kingdom of God in their hearts!

The Greek preposition can mean "within," "among," or "in the midst of." Jesus was saying, "Don't look for the kingdom 'out there' unless it is first in your own heart" (see Rom. 14:17). At the same time, He may also have been saying, "The fact that I am here in your midst is what is important, for I am the King. How can you enter the kingdom if you reject the King?" (See 19:38-40.) The Pharisees were preoccupied with the great events of the future but were ignoring the opportunities of the present (12:54-57).

Having answered the Pharisees, Jesus then turned to His disciples to instruct them about the coming of the kingdom. He warned them not to become so obsessed with His return that they end up doing nothing else but trying to track Him down. This is a good warning to believers who do nothing but study prophecy. Certainly we should look for His return and long to see Him come, but at the same time, we should be busy doing His work when He comes (note Acts 1:6-11).

To begin with, His coming will affect the whole world, so it is foolish for anyone to follow false prophets who say "He is here!" or "He is there!" Furthermore, His coming will be as sudden as a flash of lightning (Matt. 24:27, 30). While a study of the prophetic Scriptures will help us understand the general characteristics of the time of His coming, we cannot know the day or the hour (12:40, 46; Matt. 25:13). It is futile to investigate signs and try to calculate the day of His coming.

Jesus then used two Old Testament events to illustrate the certainty and the suddenness of His coming: the Flood (Gen. 6-8) and the destruction of Sodom (Gen. 19). In both examples, the people of the world were caught unprepared as they engaged in their everyday activities of eating and drinking, marrying, buying, and selling. Noah witnessed to his generation in the years preceding the Flood (2 Peter 2:5), but his preaching did not convert them. Noah and his wife, his three sons, and their wives—only eight people—were saved from destruction because they entered the ark. Peter saw this as an illustration of the salvation Christians have through faith in Jesus Christ (1 Peter 3:18-22).

Both Noah and Lot lived in days of religious compromise and moral declension, not unlike our present time. During "the days of Noah," population growth was significant (Gen. 6:1), lawlessness was on the increase (Gen. 6:5), and the earth was given over to violence (Gen. 6:11, 13). In Lot's day, the unnatural lusts of Sodom and Gomorrah were so abhorrent to God that He completely destroyed the cities. Only Lot, two of his daughters, and his wife (who later was destroyed) were saved from the terrible judgment.

Verses 30-36 describe what will occur when Jesus Christ

returns in judgment to defeat His enemies and establish His kingdom on earth (Rev. 19:11–20:6). Believers in every age of the church can take warning from these verses, but they apply in a special way to Israel at the end of the age (see Matt. 24:29-44). When Jesus comes for His church and takes it to heaven, it will happen "in a moment, in the twinkling of an eye" (1 Cor. 15:52). Nobody taking part in the rapture of the church need worry about being on a housetop or in a field and wanting to get something out of the house! However, when the Lord returns *to the earth*, His coming will first be preceded by a "sign" in heaven (Matt. 24:30-31), and some people might try to hurry home to rescue something. "Remember Lot's wife!"

The verb *taken* in verses 34-36 does not mean "taken to heaven" but "taken away in judgment" (Matt. 24:36-41). The person "left" is a believer who enters into the kingdom. Noah and his family were "left" to enjoy a new beginning, while the whole population of the earth was "taken" in the Flood. In spite of their sins, Lot and his daughters were "left" while the people in Sodom and Gomorrah were "taken" when the fire and brimstone destroyed the cities.

The fact that it is night in verse 34 but day in verses 35 and 36 indicates that the whole world will be involved in the return of Jesus Christ in glory. "Behold, He cometh with clouds; and every eye shall see Him" (Rev. 1:7).

Three times the disciples had heard Jesus talk about people being "taken" and "left," so they asked Him a most logical question: "Where, Lord?" Our Lord's reply has the sound of a familiar proverb: "Just as the eagles [and vultures, Matt. 24:28] gather at a corpse, so the lost will be gathered together for judgment." The description of the last battle in Revelation 19:17-21 certainly parallels the image of carrion-eating birds gorging themselves on flesh.

In other words, when the Lord Jesus returns to judge His

enemies, there will be a separation of the saved and the lost. Whether it be day or night, whether people are working or sleeping, the separation and judgment will come. Those who are saved will be left to enter the glorious kingdom, while those who are lost will be taken away in judgment.

Even though the primary interpretation of these verses is for Israel in the end times, they do emphasize for the church the importance of being ready when Jesus returns. We must not be like Lot's wife whose heart was so in Sodom that she looked back in spite of the angels' warning (Gen. 19:17, 26). There are many professed Christians today whose plans would be interrupted if Jesus returned! (Note 1 Thes. 5:1-11.) Our Lord's warning in verse 33 finds parallels in Matthew 10:39; Luke 9:24; and John 12:25, and is a fundamental principle of the Christian life. The only way to save your life is to lose it for the sake of Christ and the Gospel.

Jesus pictured civilization as a "rotting corpse" that would one day be ripe for judgment. The discerning believer sees evidence of this on every hand and realizes that the "days of Noah" and the "days of Lot" are soon upon us. Our Lord can return for His church at any time, so we are not looking for signs; but we do know that "coming events cast their shadows before." As we see many of these things begin to come to pass (21:28), we know that His return is nearing.

Are we looking for His return, and do we really want to see Him come?

5
People to Meet, Lessons to Learn

Luke 18

Lord Chesterfield, the English statesman, wrote, "Learning . . . is only to be acquired by reading men, and studying all the various editions of them."

He was referring to "the knowledge of the world," but what he said applies to *spiritual* knowledge as well. Much can be learned from reading the "book of humanity," whether in daily life, history, biography, or even fiction.

There are several "editions" of mankind introduced in this chapter, and each one has a spiritual lesson to teach us. Being a compassionate physician, Dr. Luke wrote about widows and politicians, Pharisees and publicans, little children and adults, rich men and beggars. From this colorful cast of characters, I have selected four "editions" for us to "read." The lessons they teach us are important.

1. A Demanding Widow (18:1-8)
Luke mentions widows more than do all the other Gospel writers combined (2:37-38; 4:25-26; 7:11-17; 18:1-8; 20:45-47; 21:1-4). In that day, widows usually had a difficult time mak-

ing ends meet, in spite of the care God instructed His people to give them (Ex. 22:22-24; Deut. 14:28-29; 16:9-15; Ps. 146:9; Isa. 1:17, 23; Jer. 7:6). The early church was serious about the care of Christian widows (Acts 6:1; 1 Tim. 5:3-10; James 1:27), a good example for us to follow today.

As you study this parable, try to see it in its Eastern setting. The "courtroom" was not a fine building but a tent that was moved from place to place as the judge covered his circuit. The judge, not the law, set the agenda; and he sat regally in the tent, surrounded by his assistants. Anybody could watch the proceedings from the outside, but only those who were approved and accepted could have their cases tried. This usually meant bribing one of the assistants so that he would call the judge's attention to the case.

The widow had three obstacles to overcome. First, being a woman she, therefore, had little standing before the law. In the Palestinian society of our Lord's day, women did not go to court. Since she was a widow, she had no husband to stand with her in court. Finally, she was poor and could not pay a bribe even if she wanted to. No wonder poor widows did not always get the protection the law was supposed to afford them!

Now that we understand something of the setting of this parable, we can better understand what Jesus was teaching. Basically, He was encouraging His disciples to pray, and He did this by presenting three contrasts.

Praying contrasted with fainting (v. 1). If we don't pray, we will faint; it's as simple as that! The word *faint* describes a believer who loses heart and gets so discouraged that he or she wants to quit. I can recall two occasions when I have fainted physically, and it is the most helpless feeling I have ever experienced. I felt myself "going," but I couldn't seem to do a thing about it!

There is a connection between what our Lord said in 18:1

and His statement in 17:37. If society is like a rotting corpse, then the "atmosphere" in which we live is being slowly polluted, and this is bound to affect our spiritual lives. But when we pray, we draw upon the "pure air" of heaven, and this keeps us from fainting.

But what does it mean "always to pray" or to "pray without ceasing"? (1 Thes. 5:17) It certainly doesn't mean that we should constantly be repeating prayers, because Jesus warned against that kind of praying (Matt. 6:5-15). Rather, it means to make prayer as natural to us as our regular breathing. Unless we are sick or smothering, we rarely think about our breathing; we just do it. Likewise with prayer—it should be the natural habit of our lives, the "atmosphere" in which we constantly live.

Prayer is much more than the words of our lips; it is the desires of our hearts, *and our hearts are constantly "desiring" before Him,* even if we never speak a word. So, to "pray without ceasing" means to have such holy desires in our hearts, in the will of God, that we are constantly in loving communion with the Father, petitioning Him for His blessing.

Take your choice: do you want to pray—or faint?

The widow contrasted with God's elect. Jesus did not say that God's people are like this woman; in fact, He said just the opposite. Because we are *not* like her, we should be encouraged in our praying. He argued from the lesser to the greater: "If a poor widow got what she deserved from a selfish judge, how much more will God's children receive what is right from a loving Heavenly Father!"

Consider the contrasts. To begin with, the woman was a stranger, *but we are the children of God,* and God cares for His children (11:13). The widow had no access to the judge, but God's children have an open access into His presence and may come at any time to get the help they need (Eph. 2:18 and 3:12; Heb. 4:14-16 and 10:19-22).

The woman had no friend at court to help get her case on the docket. All she could do was walk around the outside the tent and make a nuisance of herself as she shouted at the judge. But when Christian believers pray, they have in heaven a Saviour who is Advocate (1 John 2:1) and High Priest (Heb. 2:17-18), who constantly represents them before the throne of God.

When we pray, we can open the Word and claim the many promises of God, but the widow had no promises that she could claim as she tried to convince the judge to hear her case. We not only have God's unfailing promises, but we also have the Holy Spirit, who assists us in our praying (Rom. 8:26-27).

Perhaps the greatest contrast is that the widow came to a court of law, but God's children come to a throne of grace (Heb. 4:14-16). She pled out of her poverty, but we have all of God's riches available to us to meet our every need (Phil. 4:19). The point is clear: if we fail to pray, our condition spiritually will be just like that of the poor widow. That should encourage us to pray!

The judge contrasted with the Father. Unless you see that Jesus is pointing out contrasts, you will get the idea that God must be "argued" or "bribed" into answering prayer! God is *not* like this judge; for God is a loving Father, who is attentive to our every cry, generous in His gifts, concerned about our needs, and ready to answer when we call. The only reason the judge helped the widow was because he was afraid she would "weary" him, which literally means "give me a black eye"—i.e., ruin his reputation. God answers prayer for His glory and for our good, and He is not vexed when we come.

How, then, do we explain *delays* in answers to prayer, especially when Jesus said that God would "avenge [give them justice] speedily"? (v. 8) Remember that God's delays are not the delays of inactivity but of preparation. God is always answering prayer, otherwise Romans 8:28 could not be in the Bible. God works in all things at all times, causing all things to work together to accomplish His purposes. The moment we send Him a request that is in His will (see 1 John 5:14-15), God begins to work. We may not see it now, but one day the answer will come.

The question in verse 8 ties in with what Jesus taught in 17:22-37: "Shall He find [that kind of] faith on the earth?" The end times will not be days of great faith. Eight people were saved in Noah's day, and only four out of Sodom (and one of them perished on the way). Passages like 1 Timothy 4 and 2 Timothy 3 paint a dark picture of the last days.

2. A Deluded Pharisee (18:9-14)

Throughout His public ministry, Jesus exposed the self-righteousness and unbelief of the Pharisees (see 11:39-54). He pictured them as debtors too bankrupt to pay what they owed God (7:40-50), guests fighting for the best seats (14:7-14), and sons proud of their obedience but unconcerned about the needs of others (15:25-32). The sad thing is that the Pharisees were completely deluded and thought they were right and Jesus was wrong. This is illustrated in this parable.

The Pharisee was deluded about prayer, for he prayed with himself and told God (and anybody else listening) how good he was. The Pharisees used prayer as a means of getting public recognition and not as a spiritual exercise to glorify God (Matt. 6:5 and 23:14).

He was deluded about himself, for he thought he was accepted by God because of what he did or what he did not do. The Jews were required to fast only once a year, on the Day of Atonement (Lev. 16:29), but he fasted twice a week. He tithed everything that came into his possession, even the tiny herbs from his garden (Matt. 23:23).

He was deluded about the publican who was also in the temple praying. The Pharisee thought that the publican was a great sinner, but the publican went home justified by God while the proud Pharisee went home only self-satisfied. To be "justified" means to be declared righteous by God on the basis of the sacrifice of Jesus Christ on the cross (Rom. 3:19–4:25).

The publican repeatedly smote his breast, for he knew where his greatest problem was, and he called to God for mercy. The publican knew the enormity of his sins, but the Pharisee was blissfully ignorant of his own heart. The Pharisee's pride condemned him, but the publican's humble faith saved him (see 14:11 and Isa. 57:15). It is the prodigal son and elder brother over again (Luke 15:11ff).

In contrast to the proud Pharisee are the children who were brought to Jesus (vv. 15-17). It was customary for the Jews to bring little children to the rabbis to receive their special blessing, so it is strange that the disciples would stand in the way. Perhaps they thought Jesus was weary and needed rest, or they may have decided that He was not really interested in children. How wrong they were!

However, this was not the first time the disciples had attempted to "get rid of" people. They wanted to send the crowd away hungry, but Jesus fed them (Matt. 14:15ff); and they tried to stop the Canaanite woman from asking Jesus to heal her daughter (Matt. 15:21ff), but Jesus answered her prayer. The Twelve did not yet have the compassion of their Master, but it would come in due time.

Jesus wants us to be *childlike* but not *childish*. An unspoiled child illustrates humility, faith, and dependence. A child has a sense of wonder that makes life exciting. The only way to enter God's kingdom is to become like a child and be born again (John 3). If the proud Pharisee had become like a child, he too would have gone home justified.

3. A Dishonest Youth (18:18-34)

The rich young (Matt. 19:20) ruler may be the only man in the Gospels who came to the feet of Jesus and went away in worse condition than when he came. And yet he had so much in his favor! He was moral and religious, earnest and sincere, and probably would have qualified for membership in the average church. Yet he refused to follow Jesus Christ and instead went his own way in great sorrow.

What was wrong with him? In a word: *dishonesty*. In spite of the fact that he came to the right Person, asked the right question, and received the right answer, *he made the wrong decision*. Why? Because he was not honest with God or with himself. Therefore, he would not do what he was commanded to do. He was a superficial young man who said one thing but did another. Consider the areas in which he was dishonest.

His view of Christ (vv. 18-19). The rabbis were called "Master" (Teacher), but it was most unusual for a rabbi to be called "good." The Jews reserved the word *good* for God (Pss. 25:8; 34:8; 86:5; 106:1). This explains why our Lord asked the young man what he meant, for if he really believed that Jesus was "good," *then he had to confess that Jesus was God*. By asking this question, our Lord was not denying His deity but affirming it. He was testing the young man to see if he really understood what he had just said.

His subsequent behavior proved that the young ruler did not believe that Jesus Christ was God. If he really thought he was in the presence of Almighty God, why did he argue politely about the Law, brag about his character, and then refuse to obey the Word? Surely he knew that God sees the heart and knows all things!

His view of sin (vv. 20-21). He also had a superficial view of his own sin. No doubt the young man sincerely tried to keep the Law; in fact, this may have been what brought him to the feet of Jesus (Gal. 3:24). Jesus did not quote the Law to him as a means of salvation, because obedience to the Law does not save us. He held the Law before the young man as a mirror to reveal his sins (Rom. 3:19-20; Gal. 2:21; 3:21).

But the young man looked into the mirror and would not see the stains and blemishes in his life. When Jesus quoted from the second table of the Law, He did not quote the last commandment, "Thou shalt not covet" (Ex. 20:17). Jesus knew the young man's heart, so instead of preaching to him about covetousness, He asked him to do something that a covetous person would not do.

Nobody is saved by giving all his wealth to the poor, but nobody can be saved who will not repent of his sins and turn away from them. This young man was possessed by the love of money and he would not let go.

His view of salvation (vv. 22-27). The young man thought that eternal life came to those who "did something" (v. 18), which was a typical Jewish conviction (vv. 9-12). But when Jesus gave him something to do, he refused to obey! He wanted salvation on his terms, not God's, so he turned and went away in great sorrow.

The disciples were shocked when Jesus announced that it was difficult for rich people to be saved. They were Jews and the Jews believed that riches were a mark of God's blessing. "If rich people can't be saved," they reasoned, "what hope is there for the rest of us?" John D. Rockefeller would have agreed with them, for he once said that riches were "a gift from heaven signifying, 'This is My beloved son, in whom I am well pleased.'"

It is not possessing riches that keeps people out of heaven, for Abraham, David, and Solomon were wealthy men. It is *being possessed* by riches and *trusting* them that makes salvation difficult for the wealthy. Wealth gives people a false sense of success and security, and when people are satisfied with themselves, they feel no need for God.

Peter's comment in verse 28 suggests that he had a rather commercial view of discipleship: "What then will there be for us?" (Matt. 19:27, NASB) Jesus promised all of them ("you" in verse 29 is plural) blessings in this life and reward in the life to come, but then He balanced His words with another announcement about His impending suffering and death. How could Peter be thinking about personal gain when his Lord was going to Jerusalem to be crucified?

The rich young ruler is a warning to people who want a Christian faith that does not change their values or upset their lifestyle. Jesus does not command every seeking sinner to sell everything and give to the poor, but He does put His finger of conviction on any area in our lives about which we are dishonest.

4. A Determined Beggar (18:35-43)

Matthew tells us that there were *two* blind beggars who met Jesus as He *left* Jericho (Matt. 20:29-30), but Luke introduces us to one blind beggar, Bartimaeus, who called out as Jesus *approached* Jericho. There were two Jerichos, the old ruined city and the new one built by Herod the Great, and they stood about a mile apart. The two men, one of whom was more outspoken, were sitting at the entrance to the new city, so there is no contradiction (note Mark 10:46).

In that day, blindness was a common affliction for which there was no cure, and all a blind person could do was beg. These two men had not been born blind, for their prayer was to "regain" their sight (v. 41, NASB, and note Matt. 20:34, NASB). They persisted in crying out to the Lord, in spite of the obstacles in their way: their inability to see Jesus, the opposition of the crowd, and our Lord's delay in responding to them. They were not going to let Jesus pass them without first pleading for mercy.

The fact that they addressed Him as "Son of David," a messianic title, indicates that these two Jewish beggars knew that Jesus could give sight to the blind (Isa. 35:5; and see Luke 4:18). Jesus responded to their faith and healed them, and what a change took place! They went from darkness to light, from begging to following Jesus, and from crying to praising the Lord. They joined the pilgrim crowd going to Jerusalem and lifted their voices in praising the Lord.

The contrast is obvious between these two beggars and the rich young ruler (vv. 18-27). The beggars were poor, yet they became rich, while the young man was rich and became eternally poor. The beggars claimed no special merit and openly admitted their need, while the young man lied about himself and bragged about his character. The young man would not believe, so he went away from Jesus very sad; but the two beggars believed in Jesus and followed Him with songs of praise. "He hath filled the hungry with good things; and the rich He hath sent empty away" (1:53).

The "human editions" we have "read" in this chapter encourage us to put our faith in Jesus Christ, no matter what others may say or do. The widow was not discouraged by the indifferent attitude of the judge, nor the publican by the hypocritical attitude of the Pharisee. The parents brought their little ones to Jesus in spite of the selfish attitude of the apostles, and the blind men came to Jesus even though the crowd told them to keep quiet and stay put. Jesus always responds to faith and rewards those who believe.

But the rich young ruler stands as a warning to all who depend on character to save them from sin. This young man shows us how close a person may come to salvation and yet turn away in unbelief. John Bunyan closed his *Pilgrim's Progress* with the warning, "Then I saw that there was a way to hell, even from the gates of heaven, as well as from the City of Destruction." Heed that warning today!

6

Jerusalem At Last!

Luke 19

When Christopher Columbus made his voyage west in 1492, he kept two log books, one of which contained falsified information. He wanted his men to believe that they were closer to land than they really were. Apparently Columbus felt that the morale of the crew was more important than the integrity of the captain.

As Jesus journeyed to Jerusalem, He told His disciples what would happen there, but they could not grasp what their Lord was saying (18:31-34). Some of the people in the crowd thought He was going to Jerusalem to deliver Israel from Roman bondage and usher in the kingdom of God. Still others followed Him just to see the next miracle He would perform.

In this chapter, Dr. Luke focuses on who Jesus really is as he presents Him in a threefold ministry.

1. The Saviour Who Seeks the Lost (19:1-10)
The name *Zaccheus* means "righteous one," but this supervisor of tax collectors was not living up to his name. Certainly the Jewish religious community in Jericho would not have

71

considered him righteous, for he not only collected taxes from his own people but also worked for the unclean Gentiles! And publicans were notorious for collecting more taxes than required; the more money they collected, the more income they enjoyed (3:12-13). Though Zaccheus was a renegade in the eyes of the Jews, he was a precious lost sinner in the eyes of Jesus.

It is interesting to see the changes Zaccheus experienced that day, all because Jesus visited Jericho.

A man became a child. In the East, it is unusual for a man to run, especially a wealthy government official; yet Zaccheus ran down the street like a little boy following a parade. And he even climbed a tree! Curiosity is certainly characteristic of most children, and Zaccheus was motivated by curiosity that day.

John Calvin wrote, "Curiosity and simplicity are a sort of preparation for faith." This is often the case, and it was certainly true of Zaccheus. Why the big crowd? Who is this Jesus of Nazareth they are following? What am I missing?

Jesus said, "Whosoever shall not receive the kingdom of God like a little child shall in no way enter therein" (18:17). Perhaps more than anything else, it is pride that keeps many "successful" people from trusting Jesus Christ.

A seeking man became found. Zaccheus thought he was seeking Jesus (v. 3), but Jesus was seeking him! (v. 10) By nature, the lost sinner does not seek the Saviour (Rom. 3:11). When our first parents sinned, they hid from God, but God came and sought them (Gen. 3:1-10). When Jesus was ministering on earth, He sought out the lost; and today the Holy Spirit, through the church, is searching for lost sinners.

We do not know how God had worked in the heart of Zaccheus to prepare him for this meeting with Jesus. Was Levi, the former publican (5:27-39), one of his friends? Had he told Zaccheus about Jesus? Was he praying for Zaccheus?

Had Zaccheus become weary of wealth and started yearning for something better? We cannot answer these questions, but we can rejoice that a seeking Saviour will always find a sinner who is looking for a new beginning.

A small man became big. It was not Zaccheus' fault that he was "little of stature" and could not see over the crowd. He did what he could to overcome his handicap by putting aside his dignity and climbing a tree. In a spiritual sense, all of us are "little of stature," for "all have sinned and come short of the glory of God" (Rom. 3:23). No one measures up to God's high standards; we are all "too little" to enter into heaven.

The tragedy is, many lost sinners think they are "big." They measure themselves by man's standards—money, position, authority, popularity—things that are an "abomination in the sight of God" (16:15). They think they have everything when really they have nothing (Rev. 3:17).

Zaccheus trusted Jesus Christ and became a true "son of Abraham," meaning, of course, a child of faith (Rom. 4:12; Gal. 3:7). That is as big as you can get!

A poor man became rich. The people thought Zaccheus was a wealthy man, but actually he was only a bankrupt sinner who needed to receive God's gift of eternal life, the most expensive gift in the world. This is the only instance in the four Gospels of Jesus inviting Himself to someone's home, and it illustrates the words of Revelation 3:20.

Zaccheus was not saved because he promised to do good works. He was saved because he responded by faith to Christ's gracious word to him. Having trusted the Saviour, he then gave evidence of his faith by promising to make restitution to those he had wronged. Saving faith is more than pious words and devout feelings. It creates a living union with Christ that results in a changed life (James 2:14-26).

Under the Mosaic Law, if a thief voluntarily confessed his crime, he had to restore what he took, add one-fifth to it, and bring a trespass offering to the Lord (Lev. 6:1-7). If he stole something he could not restore, he had to repay fourfold (Ex. 22:1); and if he was caught with the goods, he had to repay double (Ex. 22:4). Zaccheus did not quibble over the terms of the Law; he offered to pay the highest price because his heart had truly been changed.

The child of God is born rich, for he shares "every spiritual blessing" in Jesus Christ (Eph. 1:3). We have the riches of God's mercy and grace (Eph. 1:7; 2:4) as well as the riches of His glory (Phil. 4:19) and wisdom (Rom. 11:33). These are "unsearchable riches" that can never be fully understood or completely exhausted (Eph. 3:8).

The host became the guest. Jesus invited Himself to Zaccheus' house, and Zaccheus received Him joyfully. *Joy* is one of the key themes in the Gospel of Luke, and the word is found over twenty times in one form or another. The experience of salvation certainly ought to produce joy in the believer's heart.

Zaccheus became the guest in his own house, for Jesus was now his Master. He was ready to obey the Lord and do whatever was necessary to establish a genuine testimony before the people. To be sure, the people criticized Jesus for visiting in a publican's house (5:27-32), but the Lord paid no attention to their words. The critics also needed to be saved, but there is no evidence that they trusted Jesus.

When a day begins, you never know how it will end. For Zaccheus, that day ended in joyful fellowship with the Son of God, for he was now a changed man with a new life. Jesus is still seeking the lost and yearning to save them. Has He found you?

2. The Master Who Rewards the Faithful (19:11-27)

Passover season was always an emotionally charged time for the Jews, because it reminded them of their deliverance from the slavery of Egypt. This annual celebration aggravated the misery of their bondage to Rome and made them yearn all the more for a deliverer. Of course, there were subversive groups like the Zealots who used commando tactics against Rome, and politicians like the Herodians who compromised with Rome, but most of the Jews rejected those approaches. They wanted God to fulfill the Old Testament prophecies and send them their promised king.

Jesus knew that many of the people in the crowd were hoping to see Him establish the kingdom, so He gave this parable to clarify things. Many of the people who listened no doubt connected it with an event in Jewish history that had occurred many years before. When Herod the Great died in 4 B.C., he left Judea to his son Archelaus, who had to go to Rome to have the inheritance approved. Not wanting Archelaus as their ruler, the Jews sent fifty men to argue their case before Augustus Caesar, who did ratify the inheritance without giving Archelaus the title of "king."

Jesus explained that the kingdom would not come until a future time, but that His servants had better be faithful now to do the job assigned to them. In the parable, you see three different responses to the Master.

Faithful obedience. Each of the servants received an amount of money equal to three months' wages for a laboring man, so you can figure out its buying power today. *Occupy* means "do business, put my money to work." They could give the money to investors and earn interest, or purchase goods and sell them for a profit. The important thing was that they give back to their master more than he had given to them. How they did it was up to them, so long as it was legal and profitable.

We are given a report on only three of the ten servants, and the first two proved to be successful. The first servant brought ten pounds more, the second brought five pounds more, and both were rewarded accordingly. These men did their job faithfully even though they were promised no rewards and had no assurance that their master would even return, let alone secure the kingdom that he sought.

The Parable of the Talents (Matt. 25:14-30) is similar to the Parable of the Pounds, but their lessons must not be confused. In this parable, each of the ten servants received the same amount but different rewards, while in the Parable of the Talents, the servants received different amounts but the same reward, the approval and joy of the Lord (Matt. 25:21).

The Parable of the Talents teaches us to be faithful to use our different gifts as God gives us opportunities to serve. Some people have a great deal of ability, so God gives them greater opportunity. The important thing is not how much ability you have but how faithful you are to use what you have for the Lord. The person with the least ability, if he or she is faithful, will receive the same reward as the most gifted church leader.

In the Parable of the Pounds, each servant has the same deposit, which probably represents the message of the Gospel (1 Thes. 2:4; 1 Tim. 1:11; 6:20). Our gifts and abilities are different, but our job is the same: to share the Word of God so that it multiplies and fills the world (1 Thes. 1:8; 2 Thes. 3:1). Only 120 believers met together on the Day of Pentecost (Acts 1:15), but before that day ended, there were 3,000 more. And before long, there were 5,000 believers (Acts 2:41). In time, the Jewish leaders accused the disciples of "filling Jerusalem" with the message! (Acts 5:28)

When it comes to witnessing, all believers start on the same level, so the reward is according to faithfulness and achievement. The faithful servants were rewarded by being made *rulers* of various cities. The reward for faithful work is always—more work! But what a compliment to be entrusted with the management of so many cities! How we serve the Lord today will help determine our reward and ministry when He comes to establish His kingdom on earth. Faithfulness now is preparation for blessed service then.

Unfaithful disobedience. At least one of the ten men did not obey his master and as a result lost even the pound that the master gave him. It is a basic principle of the Christian life that wasted opportunity means loss of reward *and possibly loss of the privilege of service.* If we do not use the gifts God gives us under His direction, why should we even have them? Somebody else can make better use of the gifts to the glory of God (see Matt. 13:12 and Luke 8:18).

"It is always so," wrote Charles Haddon Spurgeon; "the gracious and faithful man obtains more grace and more means of usefulness; while the unfaithful man sinks lower and lower and grows worse and worse. We must either make progress or else lose what we have attained. There is no such thing as standing still in religion."

This servant was unfaithful because his heart was not right toward his master. He saw his master as a hard man who was demanding and unfair. The servant had no love for his master; in fact, he feared him and dreaded to displease him. Rather than lose the pound and incur his master's anger, he guarded it so that he would at least have something to give the master if he returned and asked for a reckoning.

It is sad when a Christian is motivated by slavish fear instead of loving faith. While there is a proper "fear of the Lord" that should be in every Christian's heart, that "fear" should be the respect of a loving child and not the dread of a frightened slave. "Nothing twists and deforms the soul more than a low or unworthy conception of God," wrote Dr. A. W. Tozer. How important it is that we do the will of God from our hearts (Eph. 6:6).

Outright rebellion. The "citizens" or "enemies" are mentioned at the beginning and the ending (vv. 14, 27) and are an important part of the story, for most of the people in the crowd that day were in that category. Jesus was near Jerusalem, and in a few days He would hear the mob shout, "We have no king but Caesar!" (John 19:15) In other words, "We will not have this man to reign over us!"

God was gracious to Israel and gave the nation nearly forty years of grace before judgment fell (vv. 41-44). But we must be careful to see in this a warning to all who reject Jesus Christ—Jew or Gentile—for during this time while He is away in heaven, Jesus Christ is calling men everywhere to repent and submit to Him.

The faithful servants obeyed because they trusted their master and wanted to please him. The unfaithful servant disobeyed because he feared his master. But these citizens rebelled because they hated their king (v. 14). Jesus quoted Psalm 69:4 and told His disciples, "They hated Me without a cause" (John 15:25).

We are living today in the period between verses 14 and 15 when our Master is absent but will return according to His promise. We have been given a task to perform, and we must be faithful until He comes. What will the King say to us when He returns? Will His words mean reward, rebuke, or possibly retribution? "Moreover it is required in stewards, that a man be found faithful" (1 Cor. 4:2).

3. The King Who Offers Peace (19:28-48)
The traditional calendar for the events of our Lord's last week of ministry looks like this:

Sunday—Triumphal Entry into Jerusalem
Monday—Cleansing the temple
Tuesday—Controversies with the Jewish leaders
Wednesday—Apparently a day of rest
Thursday—Preparation for Passover
Friday—Trial and Crucifixion
Saturday—Jesus rests in the tomb
Sunday—Jesus raised from the dead

Keep in mind that the Jewish day went from sundown to sundown, so that our Thursday evening would be their Friday, the Day of Passover.

Preparation (vv. 28-36). The owners of the donkey and the colt were disciples of the Lord and had everything ready for Him. The plan was executed quietly because the Jewish leaders had let it be known that anyone confessing Christ would be excommunicated (John 9:22). The fact that the rulers planned to kill Jesus made it even more important that the owners be protected (John 7:1, 19, 25; 8:37; 11:47-57).

We think of the donkey as a lowly animal, but to the Jew it was a beast fit for a king (1 Kings 1:33, 44). Jesus rode the colt (v. 35) while the mother walked along with it. The fact that the colt had never been ridden and yet submitted to Jesus indicates our Lord's sovereignty over His creation. The laying of garments on the animals and on the road and the waving and spreading of branches were all part of a traditional Jewish reception for royalty.

Celebration (vv. 37-40). This is the only time that Jesus permitted a public demonstration on His behalf, and He did so for at least two reasons. First, He was fulfilling prophecy and presenting Himself as Israel's king (Zech. 9:9). How much of this the crowd really understood we cannot tell, even though they responded by quoting their praises from a messianic psalm (118:25-26). No doubt many of the Passover pilgrims thought that Jesus would now get rid of the Roman invaders and establish the glorious kingdom.

The second reason for this demonstration was to force the Jewish religious leaders to act. They had hoped to arrest Him *after* the Passover (Matt. 26:3-5), but God had ordained that His Son be slain *on* Passover as the "Lamb of God, who taketh away the sin of the world" (John 1:29; and see 1 Cor. 5:7). Every previous attempt to arrest Jesus had failed because "His hour had not yet come" (John 7:30; 8:20; also see John 13:1;

17:1). When they saw this great public celebration, the leaders knew that they had to act, and the willing cooperation of Judas solved their problem for them (Matt. 26:14-16).

The theme of the celebration was *peace*. Dr. Luke opened his Gospel with the angel's announcement of "peace on earth" (2:14), but now the theme was "peace in heaven." Because the King was rejected, there could be no peace on earth. Instead, there would be constant bitter conflict between the kingdom of God and the kingdom of evil (12:49-53). There would be no peace on earth but, thanks to Christ's work on the cross, there is "peace with God" in heaven (Rom. 5:1; Col. 1:20). The appeal today is, "Be ye reconciled to God!" (2 Cor. 5:17-21)

Lamentation (vv. 41-44). While the crowd was rejoicing, Jesus was weeping! This is the second occasion on which our Lord wept openly, the first being at the tomb of Lazarus (John 11:35). There He wept quietly, but here He uttered a loud lamentation like one mourning over the dead. In this, He was like the Prophet Jeremiah who wept bitterly over the destruction of Jerusalem (Jer. 9:1ff; see also the Book of Lamentations). Jonah looked upon Nineveh and hoped it would be destroyed (Jonah 4), while Jesus looked at Jerusalem and wept because it had destroyed itself.

No matter where Jesus looked, He found cause for weeping. If He looked *back*, He saw how the nation had wasted its opportunities and been ignorant of their "time of visitation." If He looked *within*, He saw spiritual ignorance and blindness in the hearts of the people. They should have known who He was, for God had given them His Word and sent His messengers to prepare the way.

As He looked *around*, Jesus saw religious activity that accomplished very little. The temple had become a den of thieves, and the religious leaders were out to kill Him. The city was filled with pilgrims celebrating a festival, but the hearts of the people were heavy with sin and life's burdens.

As Jesus looked *ahead*, He wept as He saw the terrible judgment that was coming to the nation, the city, and the temple. In A.D. 70, the Romans would come and, after a siege of 143 days, kill 600,000 Jews, take thousands more captive, and then destroy the temple and the city. Why did all of this happen? Because the people did not know that God had visited them! "He came unto His own, and His own received Him not" (John 1:11). "We will not have this man to reign over us!" (v. 14).

Denunciation (vv. 45-48). Jesus lodged in Bethany that night (Matt. 21:17) and came into the city early the next morning. It was then that He cursed the fig tree (Mark 11:12-14) and cleansed the temple for the second time. (See John 2:13-22 for the record of the first cleansing of the temple.)

The Court of the Gentiles was the only place in the temple that was available to the Gentiles. There the Jews could witness to their "pagan" neighbors and tell them about the one true and living God. But instead of being devoted to evangelism, the area was used for a "religious marketplace" where Jews from other lands could exchange money and purchase approved sacrifices. The priests managed this business and made a good profit from it.

Instead of *praying* for the people, the priests were *preying* on the people! The temple was not a "house of prayer" (Isa. 56:7); it was a "den of thieves" (Jer. 7:11). Campbell Morgan reminds us that a "den of thieves" is a place where thieves *run to hide* after they have committed their wicked deeds. The religious leaders were using the services of the holy temple to cover up their sins (see Isa. 1:1-20). But before we condemn them too harshly, have we ever gone to church and participated in religious worship just to give people the impression that we were godly?

Jesus remained in the temple and used it as a gathering

place for those who needed help. He healed many who were sick and afflicted, and He taught the people the Word of God. The hypocritical religious leaders tried to destroy Him, but His hour had not yet come and they could not touch Him. In the days that followed, they argued with Him and tried to catch Him in His words (chap. 20), but they failed. When His hour had come, He would surrender to them and they would crucify Him.

The courageous Son of God had set His face like a flint and come to Jerusalem. During His last week of ministry, He would courageously face His enemies and then bravely go to the cross to die for the sins of the world.

He still summons us to *be courageous!*

7

Issues and Answers

Luke 20

Jesus had already told the Twelve to expect conflict and suffering when they arrived in the Holy City. "The Son of man must suffer many things, and be rejected of the elders and chief priests and scribes, and be slain, and be raised the third day" (9:22). Jesus knew fully what was coming, and He was not afraid.

In this chapter, you meet the three groups of religious leaders (20:1) and witness their conflict with Jesus. They challenged Him because He had cleansed the temple and called them "thieves." They tried to catch Him in His words so they could trump up some charge against Him and have Him arrested as an enemy of the state.

But there was more to this series of questions than mere guile. The word translated "rejected" in Luke 9:22 (and also 20:17) means "to reject after investigation." It was required that the Jews carefully examine the Passover lambs from the tenth day to the fourteenth day to make sure they had no blemishes (Ex. 12:1-6). Jesus Christ, the Lamb of God (John 1:29), was watched and tested by His enemies during that final week; and yet in spite of what they saw and learned, they rejected Him.

However, *Jesus was also examining them!* For as they questioned Him, He questioned them, and their responses revealed the ignorance, hatred, and unbelief of their hearts.

Our Lord's questions centered on four different men.

1. A Question about John the Baptist (20:1-19)

The cleansing of the temple was a dramatic event that both captured the attention of the people and aroused the anger of the religious establishment. The fact that Jesus daily made the temple His headquarters for ministry only made the members of the Sanhedrin more indignant, so they decided to question Him. "What authority do You have to do these things?" they asked. "And if You do have authority, who gave it to You?"

Authority is important for the success of any social, political, or religious organization; without authority, you have confusion. The chief priests claimed their authority from Moses, for the Law set the tribe of Levi apart to serve in the sanctuary. The scribes were students of the Law and claimed their authority from the rabbis whose interpretations they studied. The elders of Israel were the leaders of the families and clans, chosen usually for their experience and wisdom. All of these men were sure of their authority and were not afraid to confront Jesus.

They wanted to push our Lord into a dilemma so that no matter how He answered, He would be in trouble. If He said that He had *no* authority, then He was in trouble with the Jews for invading their temple and acting like a prophet. If He said that His authority came from God, then He would be in trouble with the Romans who were always alert to would-be Messiahs, especially during Passover season (see Acts 5:34-39; 21:37-39).

Note our Lord's wise approach as He turned things around

and put them completely on the defensive. First, *He asked a question* (vv. 3-8); then *He gave a parable* (vv. 9-16); and finally, *He quoted a prophecy* (vv. 17-18). In each of these approaches, He revealed the sins of the nation of Israel.

Their past rejection (vv. 3-8). Jesus took them back to John the Baptist for two reasons. First, John had pointed to Jesus and introduced Him to the nation (John 1:15-34), so their rejection of John was actually a rejection of the Lord Jesus Christ. Second, it is a spiritual principle that if we disobey truth we already know, God cannot reveal new truth to us (see John 7:14-17). Why answer their question when they had refused to submit to John's message?

Now it was the religious leaders who were in the dilemma! No matter what answer they gave, they were in trouble, so they decided to "play dumb" and not answer at all. They were deceitful in asking the question and dishonest in the way they avoided answering it. Even if Jesus *had* given them an answer, *their hearts were not prepared to receive it.* If they had disobeyed God's message given by John the Baptist (7:24-30), they would disobey the message given by God's Son. That was the theme of the parable Jesus told.

Their present rebellion (vv. 9-16). These men knew the Scriptures and recognized that Jesus was speaking about the "vineyard" of Israel (Isa. 5:1-7; Ps. 80:8ff). God the Father blessed the nation abundantly and gave the Jews a land that was rich and pleasant. All He asked was that they obey His statutes and give Him the "spiritual harvest" He deserved.

Instead of being grateful for their blessings and joyfully giving the Lord His due, the nation proceeded to rob God and reject His messengers (see Neh. 9:26; Jer. 7:25-26; and 25:4). God was patient and sent them one servant after another, but they refused to obey (Matt. 23:29-39). Finally, He sent His beloved Son (3:22) and they killed Him. In this story, Jesus gave His own death announcement.

Under Jewish law, any man could lay claim to ownerless property. The tenants may have concluded that the owner was dead; otherwise he would have come himself. If they killed the son, then they could claim the vineyard for themselves. *This is exactly the way the religious leaders were thinking as they stood there before Jesus!* (See John 11:47-54.)

Their future ruin (vv. 17-18). Jesus fixed a steady gaze upon them and quoted Psalm 118:22. The rulers knew that this was a messianic psalm, and they had heard it shouted by the crowd when Jesus rode into the city (19:38 with Ps. 118:26). By applying this verse to Himself, Jesus was clearly claiming to be the Messiah. The "builders," of course, were the Jewish religious leaders (Acts 4:11).

In the Old Testament, the "stone" is a familiar symbol of God and of the promised Messiah (see Gen. 49:24; Ex. 17:6; 33:22; Deut. 32:4, 15, 30-31; Isa. 8:14; 28:16; 1 Cor. 10:4). Because the Jews did not believe, they stumbled over Him and were judged. Those who trust Jesus Christ find Him to be the foundation stone and the chief cornerstone of the church (1 Cor. 3:11; Eph. 2:20).

But Jesus also referred to Daniel 2:34-35 and 44-45, where the Messiah is pictured as a "smiting stone" that crushes all that gets in its way. He was warning the Sanhedrin that they would only destroy themselves if they condemned Him. The same principle applies today, and unbelievers should carefully heed His warning.

When the rulers rejected John the Baptist, they sinned against the Father who sent Him. When they crucified Jesus, they sinned against the Son. Jesus had told them that they could sin against Him and still be forgiven, but when they sinned against the Holy Spirit, there could be no forgiveness (Matt. 12:24-37). Why? *Because that was the end of God's witness to the nation.* This is the so-called "unpardonable sin," and it was committed by the Jewish leaders when they finally rejected the witness of the Spirit of God through the apostles. The evidence of their rejection was the stoning of Stephen (Acts 7:51-60). Then the Gospel went from the Jews to the Samaritans (Acts 8) and then to the Gentiles (Acts 10).

In this parable, Jesus illustrated the insidious nature of sin: *the more we sin, the worse it becomes.* The tenants started off beating some of the servants and wounding others, but they ended up becoming murderers! The Jewish leaders *permitted* John the Baptist to be killed, they *asked* for Jesus to be crucified, and then *they themselves stoned Stephen.* They sinned against the Father and the Son and the Holy Spirit, and that was the end of God's witness to them.

It is a serious thing to reject the message of God and the messengers of God (see Heb. 2:1-4; John 12:35-43).

2. A Question about Caesar (20:20-26)
Jesus knew that the men who questioned Him were spies sent by the Pharisees and the Herodians (Mark 12:13), but He patiently listened and replied. These two groups were usually fighting each other, but now they had a common enemy, and this brought them together. They wanted to discuss taxes and Roman authority, hoping to provoke Jesus into offending either the Jews ("Pay the poll tax!") or the Romans ("Don't pay the poll tax!"). But Jesus lifted the discussion to a much higher level and forced the spies to think about the relationship between the kingdom of God and the kingdoms of men.

Governmental authority is instituted by God and must be respected (Prov. 8:15; Dan. 2:21, 37-38; Rom. 13; 1 Peter 2:11-17). Yes, our citizenship is in heaven (Phil. 3:20), and we are strangers and pilgrims on earth, but that does not mean we should ignore our earthly responsibilities. Human government is essential to a safe and orderly society, for man is a sinner and must be kept under control.

Jesus was not suggesting that we divide our loyalties between God and government. Since "the powers that be are ordained of God" (Rom. 13:1), *we live as good citizens when we obey the authorities for the Lord's sake.* When obedience to God conflicts with obedience to man, then we must put God first (Acts 4:19-20; 5:29), but we must do it in a manner that is honorable and loving. Even if we cannot respect the people in office, *we must respect the office.* The counsel that Jeremiah gave to the Jewish exiles in Babylon is a good one for God's "strangers and pilgrims" to follow today (Jer. 29:4-7): "Seek the peace of the city!"

Caesar's image and name were on the coins, so it was basically *his* currency. To pay the poll tax meant simply to give Caesar back that which belonged to him. God's image is stamped on us; therefore, He has the right to command our lives as citizens in His kingdom. We should seek to be such good citizens that God will be glorified and the unsaved will be attracted to the Gospel and want to become Christians (1 Peter 2:9-12; 3:8-17).

It is unfortunate that some Christians have the mistaken idea that the more obnoxious they are as citizens, the more they please God and witness for Christ. We must never violate our conscience, but we should seek to be peacemakers and not troublemakers. Daniel is an example to follow (Dan. 1).

3. A Question about Moses (20:27-40)

Next in line were the Sadducees with a hypothetical question based on the Jewish law of "levirate marriage" (Gen. 38; Deut. 25:5-10). The word *levirate* comes from the Latin *levir*, which means "a husband's brother." The Sadducees accepted as Scripture only the Five Books of Moses, and they did not believe in angels, spirits, or the resurrection of the dead (Acts 23:8). They claimed that Moses did not write about any of these doctrines. The priestly party in Israel was composed of Sadducees, which explains why the priests opposed the apostles' preaching of the resurrection (Acts 4:1-2) and why they wanted to kill Lazarus, who was raised from the dead (John 12:10-11).

Jesus pointed out that His opponents were wrong and that their question revealed assumptions that limited God's power and denied God's Word. Resurrection is not reconstruction; it is the miraculous granting of a new body that has continuity with the old body but not identity. Paul compared our present body to a planted seed and the future resurrection body to the glorious flower and fruit (1 Cor. 15:35-50). Our Lord's resurrection body was the same as before His death and yet different! His friends recognized Him and even felt Him; He could eat food and yet He could also walk through doors, change His appearance, and vanish suddenly.

The future life with God is not a mere continuation of the present life only on "a higher scale." We will maintain our identities and know each other, but there will be no more death—hence, no need for marriage and procreation. Christians do not become angels. In heaven we will share the image of Jesus Christ and be much higher than the angels (1 John 3:2). Angels appear in Scripture as men, but they are spirit beings without sexuality. It is in this regard that we will be like them; there will be no marriage or childbearing in heaven.

Is not God powerful enough to raise the dead and give them new bodies suited to their new environment? If today He can give different bodies to the various things in creation, why can He not give people new bodies at the resurrection? (1 Cor. 15:35-44) In their attempt to be "rational," the Sadducees denied the very power of God!

But Jesus went beyond logic and referred them to the Word of God, particularly what happened to Moses as recorded in Exodus 3. There God identified Himself with Abraham, Isaac, and Jacob, and thus affirmed that these three patriarchs were very much alive. But if they were alive, then they were "out of the body," for they had died (James 2:26). There must be a real world of spirit beings or Moses would not have written these words. (By the way, Moses also affirmed the existence of angels: Gen. 19:1, 15; 28:12; 32:1.)

But Jesus said that Exodus 3:6, 15-16 taught not only the truth of life after death but also the reality of the resurrection. In what way? Not by direct statement but by inference. God is the God of the whole person—spirit, soul, and body (1 Thes. 5:23)—because He created the whole person. He does not simply "save our souls" and ignore the rest of our being. Inherent in the very nature of God's creative act is His concern for the total person. Hence, He will not keep us disembodied spirits forever but will give us glorious bodies to match our heavenly perfection.

Another factor is God's covenental relationship with the patriarchs. He made promises of earthly blessing to them and their descendants, but He cannot fulfill these promises if His people are going to live forever only as disembodied spirits. Can there be a glorious new heaven and earth but no corporeal glory for the people of God?

Jesus affirmed what the Sadducees denied: the existence of angels, the reality of life after death, and the hope of a future resurrection—and He did it with only one passage from Moses! Of course, He could have referred to other passages that teach a future resurrection, but He met His adversaries on their own ground (see Job 14:14; 19:25-27; Pss. 16:9-10; 17:15; Isa. 26:19; Ezek. 37; Dan. 12:2).

4. A Question about David (20:41-44)

While the Pharisees were still gathered together, Jesus asked them a final question: "What do you think about the Christ? Whose Son is He?" (Matt. 22:41-42, NKJV) This is the *key* question for every generation and each individual, for our salvation and eternal destiny are dependent on what we think about Christ (1 John 2:21-25; 4:1-6; 5:1).

Of course, they knew the expected reply: "The Son of David." They based this on such verses as 2 Samuel 7:13-14; Isaiah 11:1; and Jeremiah 23:5. God had ordained that the Messiah should come from the family of David and be born in David's city, Bethlehem (Micah 5:2). The fact that the Jewish people identified Jesus with Nazareth, not Bethlehem, indicates that they had not really looked into the facts connected with His birth (John 7:40-53).

Jesus then referred them to Psalm 110, which is quoted in the New Testament more than any other psalm. The Jewish religious leaders in that day identified Psalm 110 as a prophetic psalm and said that David was speaking of the Messiah. But if the Messiah is David's *Lord,* how can He be David's *son?* Here was an enigma for them to solve!

The only explanation is that Messiah must be both God and man. As eternal God, Messiah is David's Lord, but as man, He is David's son (Rom. 1:3; 9:4-5; Acts 2:32-36; 13:22-23).

On Palm Sunday, the multitudes had acclaimed Jesus as the Son of David, and He had not rebuked them (Matt. 21:9; Mark 11:10). By applying Psalm 110:1 to Himself, Jesus claimed to be Israel's promised Messiah, the Son of God.

Then why did the Pharisees not believe in Him? Because their minds were made up, their hearts were hardened, and their eyes were blind (John 12:37-50). They did not have the courage to confess the truth, and they persecuted those who did affirm faith in Jesus Christ. Christ's question silenced His enemies (Matt. 22:46) and ended their public challenges, but they would not admit defeat.

Because of their hypocrisy and dishonesty, the scribes and Pharisees were dangerous to have around, so Jesus warned the people about them (vv. 45-47, and see Matt. 23). Men see the outside, but God sees the heart (Heb. 4:12; 1 Sam. 16:7).

These religious leaders did not desire personal holiness; they wanted public recognition. Therefore, they wore special garments, expected special titles and greetings, and looked for special seats at public gatherings.

There is a double tragedy here. First of all, their deliberate hypocrisy was only a cover-up that enabled them to fool people and exploit them. Of all rackets, religious rackets are the worst. The religious leaders had turned the temple of God into a den of thieves and religious devotion into playacting. The general public actually thought that their leaders were godly men, when in reality they were defiling and destroying souls (Matt. 23:13-36).

The second tragedy is that they rejected their own Messiah and voted to crucify Him. They led the nation into ruin because they would not admit their sins and confess Jesus Christ. Keep in mind that these men were "experts" in the Bible, yet they did not apply its truths to their own lives. Their religion was a matter of external observance, not internal transformation.

At this point, according to Matthew (23:37-39), Jesus once again uttered a lamentation over the blind unbelief of the nation and their unwillingness to trust in Him.

He had given them many opportunities, but they had wasted them.

Now it was too late.

This same tragedy is reenacted today. This is why the Holy Spirit warns, "Today, if you will hear His voice, do not harden your hearts" (Heb. 3:7-8, NKJV).

"How often I wanted to ... but you were not willing!" (Matt. 23:37, NKJV)

8

Questions about Tomorrow

Luke 21

Now it was the disciples' turn to ask the questions!

It all started with the arrival in the temple of a poor widow with an offering for the Lord (vv. 1-4). Compared to the gifts of the rich men, her two copper coins seemed insignificant, but Jesus said that she gave more than all the others combined. "The widow's mite" does not represent *the least* we can give, but *the most*, our very all. When we sing, "Take my silver and my gold/Not a mite will I withhold," we are telling God that everything we have belongs to Him.

When it comes to our giving, God sees more than the *portion;* He also sees the *proportion.* Men see *what is given,* but God sees *what is left,* and by that He measures the gift and the condition of our hearts. Winston Churchill said, "We make a living by what we get, but we make a life by what we give." He may have learned that from Jesus (6:38) or perhaps from Paul (2 Cor. 8:1-15).

The temple was a beautiful structure, embellished with many costly decorations that a poor widow could never give, and the disciples mentioned this to Jesus. But our Lord was not impressed. He told them that the day would come when the beautiful Jewish temple would be demolished (vv. 5-6). He had already announced that the city would be destroyed (19:41-44), but now He specifically mentioned the destruction of the temple.

Jesus left the temple and went to the Mount of Olives, and there Peter, James, and John asked Him three questions: (1) When would the temple be destroyed? (2) What would be the sign of His coming? (3) What would be the sign of the end of the age? (See Mark 13:3-4; Matt. 24:3.) The disciples thought that these three events would occur at the same time, but Jesus explained things differently. Actually, the temple would be destroyed first, and then there would be a long period of time before He would return and establish His kingdom on earth (see 19:11-27).

Our Lord's reply comprises what we call "The Olivet Discourse," the greatest prophetic sermon He ever preached. It is recorded in greater detail in Matthew 24—25 and Mark 13, and you will want to compare the three passages. Since Luke wrote with the Gentile reader in mind, he omitted some of the strong Jewish elements of the sermon while retaining the essential truths that we must consider and apply.

Keep in mind that this was a message given to Jews by a Jew about the future of the Jewish nation. Though there are definite applications to God's people today, the emphasis is on Jerusalem, the Jews, and the temple. Our Lord was not discussing His coming for the church, for that can occur at any time and no signs need precede it (1 Thes. 4:13-18; 1 Cor. 15:51-58). "For the Jews require a sign" (1 Cor. 1:22); the church looks for a Saviour (Phil. 3:20-21).

The sermon focuses on a period in God's program called "the Tribulation" when God will pour out His wrath on the nations of the world. Many Bible students believe that the Tribulation will begin after the Lord comes *in the air* and takes His church to heaven (1 Thes. 4:13-5:11). It will climax with the return of Jesus Christ *to the earth,* at which time He will defeat His foes and establish His kingdom (Rev. 19:1–20:6).

It is helpful to see the development of the sermon as a whole, so here is a suggested outline:

> *The first half of the Tribulation*
> (Matt. 24:4-14; Mark 13:5-13; Luke 21:8-19)
> *The middle of the Tribulation*
> (Matt. 24:15-28; Mark 13:14-18; note Dan. 9:24-27)
> *The last half of the Tribulation*
> (Matt. 24:29-31; Mark 13:19-27; Luke 21:25-27)
> *Closing admonitions*
> (Matt. 24:32–25:51; Mark 13:28-37; Luke 21:28-36)

Jesus answered the disciples' questions by discussing four topics relating to the future of the nation of Israel.

1. The Description of the Age (21:8-19)
The characteristics Jesus stated can be seen in *every* age of the church, for from the beginning there have been counterfeit messiahs, national and international upheavals, and religious persecution. But these things will *increase and intensify* as the time of Jesus' coming draws near. Thomas Campbell, British poet and educator, said that "coming events cast their shadows before" and he was right.

There will be *religious delusion* (v. 8), and even God's people will be in danger of being deceived. Satan is a counterfeiter who for centuries has led people astray by deceiving their minds and blinding their hearts (2 Cor. 11:1-4, 13-15; 4:1-6). Israel was often seduced into sin by false prophets, and the church has had its share of false teachers (2 Peter 2).

Most people are naturally concerned about the future, especially when world events are threatening; therefore, religious racketeers can prey upon them and take advantage of them. In every age, there are those who either claim to be the Christ or claim to know when He will return. These false prophets often "use" the Scriptures to "prove" the accuracy of their predictions, in spite of the fact that Jesus clearly stated that nobody knows the time of His return (Matt. 24:36-44).

"Be not deceived!" is our Lord's admonition, and we must take it to heart. The only sure way to keep our balance in a deceptive world is to know the Scriptures and obey what God tells us to do (2 Peter 3:17-18). It is foolish and hurtful to become so obsessed with Bible prophecy that we start to neglect the practical things of the Christian life. Blessed are the balanced!

There will also be *international distress* (vv. 9-11). I have a friend who has been keeping track of the earthquakes that have occurred in recent years. Another prophetic student has a list of all the wars and attempted invasions. Both have overlooked the fact that Jesus said that wars, earthquakes, pestilences, and famines *by themselves* are not signs of His soon return. These things have been going on throughout the history of the world.

However, during the first half of the Tribulation, these events will multiply and intensify. Matthew 24:1-14 lists them in detail, and if you compare Revelation 6, you will see the parallel:

Events	Matthew	Revelation
false Christs	24:4-5	6:1-2
wars	24:6	6:3-4
famines	24:7a	6:5-6
death	24:7b-8	6:7-8
martyrs	24:9	6:9-11
worldwide chaos	24:10-13	6:12-17

In fact, most of Revelation, chapters 6–19, describes the Tribulation period in detail and follows the outline of Matthew 24: (1) first half of the Tribulation, vv. 6-9; (2) middle of the Tribulation, vv. 10-14; (3) last half of the Tribulation, vv. 15-19.

Our Lord's admonition to His people is, "Don't be terrified!" These things must come to pass; there is nothing anyone can do to prevent them. This does not mean that God's people are submitting to blind fate; rather, it means they are yielding to the plan of a loving Father who works all things "after the counsel of His own will" (Eph. 1:11).

Finally, there will be *religious persecution*, both official (vv. 12-15) and personal (vv. 16-19). Of course, there has been religious persecution ever since Cain killed Abel (Matt. 23:34-36; and see Acts 4:1ff; 5:17ff; 6:9ff; 8:1ff). Jesus promised that His people would suffer (John 15:18–16:4, 32-33), and that promise holds true today (2 Tim. 3:12). But the persecution in the end times will be much more severe and many will give their lives for Christ.

Notice the encouragements Jesus gives to all who suffer persecution. To begin with, we must remember that when we are persecuted, we suffer *for His name's sake* (v. 12), and this is a high honor (Acts 5:41). It is not important what people say about our names, but it is important that the name of Christ be glorified.

Second, times of suffering provide opportunities for witness (vv. 13-15). The apostles made good use of the witness stand when they were arrested and taken before the council (Acts 4–5), and Christ's servants and martyrs down through the centuries have followed their example. The English word *martyr* comes from the Greek word *martus* which means "a witness" (see 1 Peter 3:13-17).

Because of official persecution, God's witnesses will stand before important people; and when that happens, they must not panic, for God will give them the words to speak. This promise is not an excuse for lazy preachers or Sunday School teachers who do not want to study! Rather, it is an assurance to faithful witnesses that God will always give them the words they need when they need them.

Not only will the saints endure official persecution from the government, but there will also be opposition from family and friends. Relatives will even follow in the footsteps of Judas and betray their Christian loved ones to be killed. Hatred, arrest, and death will be the lot of many of God's children during the Tribulation.

But they must not despair, for God is in control. Not a hair on their head can perish apart from His sovereign will (Matt. 10:28-31). Knowing this, they can have endurance and be able to face the challenge with faith and courage.

While many Christians today enjoy freedom from official persecution, or even family opposition, there are others who suffer greatly for their faith, and what our Lord said here is an encouragement to them. A friend of mine ministered in Eastern Europe, and a believer in Poland said to him, "We are praying for you Christians in the Western world *because you have it too easy.* The Lord must help you not to compromise."

Remember, the things Jesus described here are not signs of His soon return, because they have been going on for centuries. However, as the coming of the Lord draws near, these things will multiply and intensify. No matter what our views may be of the coming of the Lord, we all need to heed His three admonitions: "Don't be deceived! Don't be afraid! Don't worry!"

2. The Destruction of the Temple (21:20-24)

This paragraph is peculiar to Luke; there is no parallel in Matthew or Mark, in spite of the similar language in Matthew

24:16-21 and Mark 13:14-17. However, it is clear that both Matthew and Mark were referring to events in the middle of the Tribulation when "the abomination of desolation" would be set up in the Jewish temple and the Antichrist (the world ruler) would begin to persecute Israel (Dan. 9:24-27; Rev. 13). Jesus warned the people to flee and go into hiding, for "great tribulation" was about to fall.

Luke's account refers not to a distant event to occur during the Tribulation but to the destruction of Jerusalem by Titus and the Roman army in A.D. 70, just forty years from that time (see 19:41-44). This terrible event was in many respects a "dress rehearsal" for what will happen when Satan vents his anger on Israel and the believing Gentiles during the last half of the Tribulation (Rev. 12:7-17). The Jewish historian Josephus claimed that over a million people were killed by the Romans, and over 100,000 taken captive, when Titus captured the city.

This was not the first time Jerusalem would be "trodden down of the Gentiles," for the Babylonians had destroyed the city in 586 B.C. when "the times of the Gentiles" began. This significant period in God's plan will end when Jesus Christ returns to the earth, destroys all Gentile power, and sets up His own righteous kingdom (Dan. 2:34-36, 44-45; Rev. 19:11ff).

Believers today who are looking for their Lord's return should not apply verses 20-24 to their own situation. Jesus was talking about Jerusalem in A.D. 70. In Matthew 24:15-28 and Mark 13:14-23, He was speaking about Israel's situation at the middle of the Tribulation. Since our Lord's coming for the church will take place "in the twinkling of an eye" (1 Cor. 15:52), no one will have time to go back home for a coat; nor will we have to worry about traveling on the Sabbath or caring for nursing babies.

Thus far in His message, our Lord has told the disciples

when the temple would be destroyed and what signs would point to the end of the age. Now He tells them about His own coming at the end of the Tribulation period.

3. The Return of the Lord (21:25-28)

Revelation 15–19 describes the frightening judgment signs that God will send on the earth during the last half of the "time of Jacob's trouble" (Jer. 30:7). When these things occur, it will be evidence that the Lord's coming is drawing near. The image of "waves roaring" describes nations rising and falling like waves in a storm (Ps. 46:1-6; Rev. 17:15). It will be an awesome time, and the population of the earth will tremble with fear, but men will not repent of their sins and turn to God by faith (Rev. 9:20-21; 16:9-11).

Matthew 24:29 informs us that the sun and moon will be darkened and the stars will fall (Isa. 13:10; 34:4; Joel 2:10, 31; 3:15). Matthew 24:30 states that "the sign of the Son of man" will appear in heaven. We do not know what this "sign" is, but it will produce fear among the nations of the earth. However, then Jesus Christ will appear, and every eye will see Him (Rev. 1:7). The nation of Israel will at last recognize their Messiah, repent, believe, and be saved (Zech. 12:10-14; and see Mark 14:61-62).

These awesome signs will bring terror to the lost people of the world, but hope to those who have trusted the Lord during the Tribulation period (Rev. 7), for these believers know that the Lord's coming will be soon. Believers today look for the Saviour, not signs. However, as we see "coming events casting their shadows," we believe that the Lord's return is near.

Christ's appearing will be sudden, glorious, and with great power (v. 27). The image here is taken from Daniel 7:13-14, a messianic passage that must have been familiar to the disciples. The angels promised that Jesus would return to earth in the same way He departed (Acts 1:9-11), and He will (Rev. 1:7).

There are those who ignore and even ridicule the doctrine of the return of Christ. After all, the church has been waiting for the Lord for 2,000 years, and He has not returned yet! Peter answered that accusation in 2 Peter 3. He pointed out that God keeps His promises whether we believe them or not, and that God measures time differently from the way men measure it. Furthermore, the reason He waits is so that *unsaved sinners may repent, be saved, and be ready when Jesus comes.* While His seeming delay is a trial to the church, it is an opportunity for the lost.

Having answered their questions, the Lord then "applied" the message to their hearts by giving them two closing admonitions: "Know!" and "Watch!"

4. The Responsibilities of the Believers (21:29-38)

In the Bible, the fig tree is often an image of Israel (13:6-10; Hosea 9:10). Some students interpret this parable to mean that the emergence of the State of Israel on May 15, 1948 was the "sign" that the Lord would soon return. Surely it is a significant thing that Israel is now a free nation after so many centuries of political bondage. But Luke added "and all the trees" (v. 29), suggesting that more than one nation is involved. Perhaps Jesus was saying that *the rise of nationalism around the world* is the thing to watch. In recent years we have certainly seen the growth of nationalism and the emerging of new nations, and this may be a "sign" that the coming of the Lord is near.

However, the basic idea here is that of *knowing what is going on.* As the budding of the trees indicates that summer is near, so the occurring of these signs indicates that the Lord's return is near (see 12:54-57 for a similar passage). The important thing is that the believer *know* that God is keeping His promises and that His Word will not fail (Josh. 23:14).

To what "generation" does verse 32 apply? Some who doubt that Jesus will literally return say that this statement applies to the generation of the apostles, so that "the coming of the Lord" was either the coming of the Spirit at Pentecost (Acts 2) or the destruction of Jerusalem in A.D. 70. *But none of the signs Jesus mentioned took place before or during those events.* Nor did they climax with the deliverance of Israel and the establishing of the kingdom.

Jesus was probably referring to the generation that would be alive on earth at the time all these things take place. He was not suggesting that it would take a whole generation to accomplish these things, for they will occur with swiftness once they begin. The Greek word translated "generation" can also mean "race" and could refer to the people of Israel. Jesus used it that way in Mark 8:12, 38 and 9:19. Jesus was assuring the disciples that, in spite of all the difficulties Israel would endure, the nation would be protected by God and not be destroyed. Satan has wanted to destroy the nation of Israel, but he will not succeed.

His first admonition was "Know!" and His second was "Watch!" (vv. 34-36) Both admonitions apply to God's people in every age, although they will have a special meaning for the Jews of the Tribulation period. "Watch!" does not mean to stand around looking for signs. It means, "Be awake! Be alert! Don't get caught unprepared!" This admonition carries a warning for us today, because it is so easy for us to "get weighted down" with the cares of this life and the temptations of the world and the flesh (see 12:35-48).

During difficult times, it is easy to give up and start living like the unsaved world; and believers during the Tribulation period will face that temptation. They must "watch and pray" and resist the temptations around them, for they want to be ready when their Lord returns.

Verse 36 refers primarily to believers standing before the Lord at the judgment when He returns to earth to establish His kingdom (Matt. 25:31-46). The sheep will enter into the kingdom while the goats will be cast out. While some of God's people will die during the Tribulation judgments and persecutions, some will "escape" and see Jesus Christ when He returns in glory.

If believers during that *difficult* age will be tempted to yield to the world and the flesh, Christians in this present age of comfort and affluence must face even greater dangers. We today do not know when our Lord will return, and it behooves us to be faithful and to be ready.

The godly Scottish Presbyterian minister Robert Murray McCheyne sometimes asked people, "Do you believe Jesus will return today?" They usually replied, "No." Then McCheyne would say, "Then you had better be ready, for He is coming at an hour you think not!"

"I'm not looking for signs," said the late Vance Havner; "I'm listening for a sound."

The sound of the trumpet! The shout of the archangel! "Even so, come, Lord Jesus!" (Rev. 22:20)

9

In the Upper Room

Luke 22:1-38

Jesus had "steadfastly set His face to go to Jerusalem" (9:51), knowing full well what would happen to Him there; and now those events were about to occur. They were appointments, not accidents, for they had been determined by the Father and written centuries ago in the Old Testament Scriptures (24:26-27). We cannot but admire our Saviour and love Him more as we see Him courageously enter into this time of suffering and eventual death. We must remember that He did it for us.

The Passover supper in the Upper Room gives us the focus for our present study.

1. Before the Supper: Preparation (22:1-13)

Passover, Pentecost, and Tabernacles were the three most important feasts on the Jewish calendar (Lev. 23); and all the Jewish men were expected to go to Jerusalem each year to celebrate (Deut. 16:16). The Feast of Passover commemorated the deliverance of Israel from Egypt, and it was a time for both remembering and rejoicing (Ex. 11–12). Thousands of excited pilgrims crowded in and around Jerusalem during that week, causing the Romans to always be nervous about possible uprisings. Passover had strong political overtones, and it was the ideal time for some would-be messiah to attempt to overthrow Rome. This explains why King Herod and Pontius Pilate, the Roman governor, were in Jerusalem instead of being at Tiberius and Caesarea respectively. They wanted to help keep the peace.

The religious leaders prepared for a crime (vv. 1-6). It is incredible that these men perpetrated history's greatest crime during Israel's holiest festival. During Passover, the Jews were expected to remove all leaven (yeast) from their houses (Ex. 12:15) as a reminder that their ancestors left Egypt in haste and had to eat unleavened bread. Jesus had warned His disciples about the "leaven of the Pharisees, which is hypocrisy" (12:1; also see Matt. 16:6; 1 Cor. 5:1-8), and now we see this hypocrisy at work.

The religious leaders had cleansed their homes but not their hearts (see Matt. 23:25-28). For a long time now, they had wanted to arrest Jesus and get Him out of the way, but they had not been able to work out a safe plan that would protect them from the people. Judas solved their problem for them. He guaranteed to deliver Jesus to them privately so there would be no uproar from the people. The last thing the Jewish Sanhedrin wanted was a messianic uprising at Passover season (see 19:11).

Judas was motivated and energized by Satan (John 13:2, 27), for he never was a true believer in Jesus Christ. His sins had never been cleansed by the Lord (John 13:10-11), and he had never believed and received eternal life (John 6:64-71). Yet none of the other apostles had the least suspicion that Judas was a traitor. We have every reason to believe that Judas had been given the same authority as the other men and that he had preached the same message and performed the same miracles. It shows how close a person can come to

God's kingdom and still be lost (Matt. 7:21-29).

Why did Judas betray the Lord Jesus? We know that he was a thief (John 12:4-6) and that money played a part in his terrible deed. But thirty pieces of silver was not a large payment for such a great crime, and there had to be something more involved. It is possible that Judas saw in Jesus the salvation of the Jewish nation and, therefore, he followed Him because he hoped to hold an office in the kingdom. Keep in mind that the Twelve often argued over who was the greatest in the kingdom, and Judas, the treasurer, surely participated in those important discussions.

When Judas understood that Jesus would not establish the kingdom but rather would surrender to the authorities, he turned against Him in bitter retaliation. The "leaven" in his life grew quietly and secretly until it produced "malice and wickedness" (1 Cor. 5:6-8). When you cooperate with Satan, you pay dearly, and Judas ended up destroying himself (Matt. 27:3-5). Satan is a liar and a murderer (John 8:44), and he reproduced himself perfectly in Judas.

Jesus prepared for the Passover (vv. 7-13). The way our Lord arranged for the Passover feast indicates that He knew there were plots afoot. Until the disciples arrived at the Upper Room, only Jesus and Peter and John had known where the feast would be held. Had Judas known, he might have been tempted to inform the authorities.

Peter and John would have no trouble locating the man with the water pitcher, because men rarely carried pitchers of water. This was the task of the women. Like the men who owned the ass and colt (19:28-34), this anonymous man was a disciple of Jesus who made his house available to the Master for His last Passover.

Peter and John would purchase an approved lamb and take it to the temple to be slain. Then they would take the lamb and the other elements of the supper to the house where they planned to meet, and there the lamb would be roasted. The table would be furnished with wine, unleavened bread, and the paste of bitter herbs that reminded the Jews of their long and bitter bondage in Egypt (see Ex. 12:1-28).

There is a chronological question here that must be addressed or it will appear that the Gospel writers are contradicting each other. According to John 18:28, the Jewish leaders had not yet eaten the Passover, and the day Jesus was tried and condemned was "the preparation of the Passover" (John 19:14). But our Lord and His disciples had already eaten the Passover!

In their excellent *Harmony of the Gospels* (Harper & Row), Robert Thomas and Stanley Gundry suggest a possible solution to the dilemma (pp. 320–23). The Jews at that time reckoned days in one of two ways: from sunset to sunset or from sunrise to sunrise. The first approach was traditionally Jewish (Gen. 1:5) while the second was Roman, although it had biblical precedent (see Gen. 8:22).

If Matthew, Mark, and Luke used the Jewish reckoning, and John the Roman, then there is no contradiction. There was an "overlapping" of days that permitted both groups to celebrate on the same *date* but a different *day*. The temple priests permitted the Jews to bring their lambs for sacrifice either the earlier or the later time. Apparently the Jewish leaders followed the Roman form of reckoning (John 18:28) while Jesus and the disciples followed the Jewish form. Our Lord was crucified on Passover at the time when the lambs were being slain, becoming a fulfillment of Old Testament type.

2. During the Supper: Revelation (22:14-16, 21-38)
The disciples did not know what to expect as they met in the Upper Room, but it turned out to be an evening of painful revelation. Jesus, the host of the supper, met them with the

traditional kiss of peace (He kissed Judas!), and then the men reclined around the table, Judas at our Lord's left and John at His right (John 13:23).

Jesus revealed His love (vv. 14-16). He did this by what He *said* and by what He *did*. He told His friends that He had a great desire to share this last Passover with them before He suffered. Passover commemorated the exodus of Israel from Egypt centuries before, but He would accomplish a greater "exodus" on the cross. He would purchase redemption from sin for a world of lost sinners (9:31).

Then He arose, girded Himself with a towel, and washed the disciples' feet, including Judas' (John 13:1-20). Later that evening, the Twelve would argue over which of them was the greatest, so this lesson on humility and service did not penetrate their hearts. Perhaps Peter had this scene in mind when years later he admonished his readers to "be clothed with humility" (1 Peter 5:5; and see Phil. 2:1-11).

Our Lord's words in verse 16 indicate that there would be no more Passover on God's calendar. The next feast would be the great "kingdom feast" when He would return to establish His rule on earth (vv. 28-30; 13:24-30; Matt. 8:11-12). He saw beyond the suffering to the glory, beyond the cross to the crown; and in His love, He reached out to include His friends.

Jesus revealed the presence of treachery (vv. 21-23). He had already hinted to His disciples that one of their number was not truly with Him (John 6:66-71), but now He openly spoke about a traitor in their midst. However, He did not do this just for the sake of the disciples, but more for the sake of Judas. Jesus had kissed Judas and washed his feet, and now He was giving Judas another opportunity to repent. It is most significant that Jesus did not openly identify Judas as the traitor but protected him until the very end.

If Jesus knew that Judas would betray Him, why did He choose him in the first place? And, if *somebody* had to betray the Lord, why condemn Judas? After all, he simply did God's will and fulfilled the Old Testament prophecy. (See Pss. 41:9; 55:12-14; compare Pss. 69:25 and 109:8 with Acts 1:15-20.)

Before He chose His twelve Apostles, Jesus spent a whole night in prayer (6:12-16), so we must believe that it was the Father's will that Judas be among them (John 8:29). But the selection of Judas did not seal his fate; rather, it gave him opportunity to watch the Lord Jesus closely, believe, and be saved. God in His sovereignty had determined that His Son would be betrayed by a friend, *but divine foreknowledge does not destroy human responsibility or accountability.* Judas made each decision freely and would be judged accordingly, even though he still fulfilled the decree of God (Acts 2:23).

The fact that the disciples were puzzled by this strange announcement reveals that they did not know Judas' true character, their own hearts ("Which of us could do such a terrible thing?"), or the prophecies in the psalms. Nor did they remember the Lord's statements that He would be betrayed into the hands of the enemy (Matt. 17:22; 20:18). If Peter had fully understood what was happening, he might have used his sword on Judas!

Much about Judas remains a mystery to us, and we must not speculate too much. Judas is certainly a witness to the sinlessness of Jesus Christ, for if anybody could have given witness against Him, it was Judas. However, the authorities had to find false witnesses in order to build their case against Jesus. Judas admitted that he had "betrayed innocent blood" (Matt. 27:4).

At this point, Judas left the Upper Room to go to the religious leaders and get ready for the arrest of Jesus in the garden. Judas went out "and it was night" (John 13:30), for he was obeying the prince of darkness (22:53). Alas, for Judas, *it is still night and always will be night!*

Jesus revealed the disciples' worldliness (vv. 24-30). This was not the first time the disciples had committed this sin (9:46-48; Matt. 20:20-28; Mark 9:33-37), but in the light of what their Lord had said and done that evening, this latest exhibition was inexcusable. Perhaps the argument grew out of their speculating over who would betray Him, or there may have been some jealousy over the way they had been seated at the table. When you are interested in promoting yourself, it doesn't take much to start an argument.

Jesus had to explain that they were thinking like the unsaved Gentiles and not like God's children. The Romans in particular vied for honors and did all they could, legally and illegally, to win promotion and recognition, but they are not the examples for us to follow. As in all things, Jesus is our example, and He has completely reversed the measure of true greatness.

True greatness means to be like Jesus, and that means being a servant to others. A servant does not argue over who is the greatest, because he knows that he is the least, and he accepts this from the hand of God. Since all Christians are to be servants, there is no reason for us to compete with one another for honors and recognition. It is too bad that this competitive spirit is so strong in the church today as people promote themselves and their ministries as "the greatest."

Jesus closed this lesson on servanthood by reminding them of their future reward in the kingdom (vv. 28-30). In spite of their weaknesses and failures, the disciples had stood by Jesus during His earthly ministry, and God would honor them for their faithfulness. We should not mind being servants today, for we shall sit on thrones in the future kingdom! For that matter, our faithful service today is preparing us for the rewards we shall receive. Jesus has set the example: first the cross, then the crown.

Jesus revealed Peter's denial (vv. 31-38). It is interesting that this word of warning followed the dispute over who was the greatest! Imagine how the disciples must have felt when they heard that not only would one of their number betray Him, but that their spokesman and leader would publicly deny Him! If a strong man like Peter was going to fail the Lord, what hope was there for the rest of them?

The word *you* in verse 31 is plural; Satan asked to have all the disciples so he might sift them like wheat. These men had been with Jesus in His trials (v. 28), and He would not forsake them in their trials. This was both a warning and an encouragement to Peter and the other men, and our Lord's prayers were answered. Peter's courage failed but not his faith; he was restored to fellowship with Christ and was greatly used to strengthen God's people.

Peter's self-confident boasting is a warning to us that none of us really knows his own heart (Jer. 17:9) and that we can fail *in the point of our greatest strength*. Abraham's greatest strength was his faith, and yet his faith failed him when he went down to Egypt and lied about Sarah (Gen. 12:10-13:4). Moses' strength was in his meekness (Num. 12:3), yet he lost his temper, spoke rashly with his lips, and was not allowed to enter Canaan (Num. 20). Peter was a brave man, but his courage failed him and he denied his Lord three times. "Therefore let him who thinks he stands take heed lest he fall" (1 Cor. 10:12, NKJV).

The word *converted* in verse 32 means "turned around." Peter was already a *saved* man, but he would soon start going in the wrong direction and would have to be turned around. He would not lose the gift of eternal life, but he would disobey the Lord and jeopardize his discipleship. Actually, all of the disciples would forsake Jesus, but Peter would also deny Him. It is a humbling lesson for all of us.

Our Lord's counsel in verses 35-38 was not fully understood by the disciples, because they interpreted what He said quite literally. Peter's use of the sword in the garden is evidence of this (vv. 49-51). The point He was making was this: "You are now moving into a whole new situation. If they arrest Me, they will one day arrest you. If they treat Me like a common criminal (Isa. 53:12), they will do the same to you; so, be prepared!"

During their ministry with Jesus, the disciples had been sent out with special authority, and they were treated with respect and appreciation (9:1ff; 10:1ff). At that time, Jesus was still a very popular rabbi, and the authorities were not able to attack His disciples. But now "His hour had come" and the situation would change radically. Today, God's people are aliens in enemy territory, and we must use our faith and sanctified common sense as we serve the Lord. This is a good warning to zealous people who foolishly get themselves into tight spots and then expect God to perform miracles for them. The Apostle Paul knew how to use the "sword" of human government to protect him and the Gospel (Rom. 13; Acts 16:35-40; 21:37-40; 25:11).

Their words "Here are two swords!" must have grieved the Lord, for they indicated that the disciples had missed the meaning of His words. Did they think that He needed their protection or that He would now overthrow Rome and establish the kingdom? "It is enough!" means "Don't say anything more about the matter" (Deut. 3:26). His kingdom does not advance by means of men's swords (John 18:36-37) but by the power of God's truth, the Word of God that is sharper than any human sword (Eph. 6:17; Heb. 4:12).

3. After the Supper: Commemoration (22:17-20)

It was when the Passover meal was drawing to a close (v. 20; Matt. 26:25) that Jesus instituted the ordinance that the church calls "The Communion" (1 Cor. 10:16), or "The Lord's Supper" (1 Cor. 11:20), or "The Eucharist," from the Greek word which means "to give thanks."

The Passover feast opened with a prayer of thanksgiving, followed by the drinking of the first of four cups of wine. (The wine was diluted with water and was not intoxicating.)

Next they ate the bitter herbs and sang Psalms 113–114. Then they drank the second cup of wine and began eating the lamb and the unleavened bread. After drinking the third cup of wine, they sang Psalms 115–118; and then the fourth cup was passed among them. It is likely that it was this fourth cup of wine that Jesus used when He instituted the Supper.

Paul gave the order of the Supper in 1 Corinthians 11:23-26. First, Jesus broke a piece from the unleavened loaf, gave thanks, and shared it with the disciples, saying that it represented His body which was given for them. He then gave thanks for the cup and shared it, saying that it represented His blood. It was a simple observance that used the basic elements of a humble Jewish meal. Jesus sanctified the simple things of life and used them to convey profound spiritual truths.

Jesus stated one of the purposes for the Supper: "in remembrance of Me" (1 Cor. 11:24-25). It is a memorial feast to remind the believer that Jesus Christ gave His body and blood for the redemption of the world. There is no suggestion in the accounts of the Supper that anything "miraculous" took place when Jesus blessed the bread and the cup. The bread remained bread and the wine remained wine, and the physical act of receiving the elements did not do anything special to the eleven disciples. When we partake, we identify ourselves with His body and blood (1 Cor. 10:16), but there is no suggestion here that we receive His body and blood.

A second purpose for the supper is the proclaiming of His death until He returns (1 Cor. 11:26). The Supper encourages us to *look back* with love and adoration to what He did for us on the cross and to *look forward* with hope and anticipation to His coming again. Since we must be careful not to come to the Lord's table with known sin in our lives, the Supper should also be an occasion for *looking within*, examining our hearts, and confessing our sins (1 Cor. 11:27-32).

A third blessing from the Supper is the reminder of the unity of the church: we are "one loaf" (1 Cor. 10:17). It is "The *Lord's* Supper" and is not the exclusive property of any Christian denomination. Whenever we share in the Supper, we are identifying with Christians everywhere and are reminded of our obligation to "keep the unity of the Spirit in the bond of peace" (Eph. 4:3).

For us to receive a spiritual blessing from the Supper, it takes more than mere physical participation. We must also be able to "discern the body" (1 Cor. 11:29), that is, see the spiritual truths that are inherent in the bread and the cup. This spiritual discernment comes through the Spirit using the Word. The Holy Spirit makes all of this real to us as we wait before the Lord at the table.

Following the instituting of the Supper, Jesus taught His disciples many of the basic truths they desperately needed to know in order to have effective ministries in a hostile world (John 14–16). He prayed for His disciples (John 17); then they sang a hymn and departed from the Upper Room for the Garden of Gethsemane. Judas knew they would go there and he would have the arresting officers all prepared.

As you review this passage, you cannot help but be impressed with the calmness and courage of the Saviour. It is He who is in control, not Satan or Judas or the Sanhedrin. It is He who encourages the apostles! And He is able even to sing a hymn before He goes out to die on a cross! Isaac Watts has best expressed what our response should be:

> Love so amazing, so divine,
> Demands my soul, my life, my all.

10

The Night They Arrested God

Luke 22:39-71

Perhaps the best way to grasp the spiritual lessons behind the tragic events of that night is to focus on the *symbols* that appear in the narrative. The Bible is a picture book as well as a book of history and biography, and these pictures can say a great deal to us. In this passage, there are six symbols that can help us better understand our Lord's suffering and death. They are: a lonely garden, a costly cup, a hypocritical kiss, a useless sword, a crowing cock, and a glorious throne.

1. A Lonely Garden (22:39)

The Son of man left the Upper Room and went with His disciples to the Garden of Gethsemane on the Mount of Olives. This was His customary place of retirement when in Jerusalem (21:37). Knowing that the Lord would be there (John 18:1-2), Judas led his band of Roman soldiers and temple guards into the garden to arrest Jesus, who willingly yielded Himself into their hands.

But why a garden? Human history began in a garden (Gen. 2:7-25) and so did human sin (Gen. 3). For the redeemed, the whole story will climax in a "garden city" where there will be no sin (Rev. 21:1–22:7). But between the garden where man failed and the garden where God reigns is Gethsemane, the garden where Jesus accepted the cup from the Father's hand.

John informs us that when Jesus went to the garden, He crossed the Kidron brook (John 18:1). John may have had in mind King David's experience when he left Jerusalem and fled from his son Absalom (2 Sam. 15; and note especially v. 23). Both David and Jesus were throneless kings, accompanied by their closest friends and rejected by their own people. The name *Kidron* means "murky, dark," and *Gethsemane* means "olive press." Surely these names are significant.

Guides in modern Jerusalem can take visitors to four different sites that lay claim to being the ancient Garden of Gethsemane. Perhaps the most widely accepted one, and surely the most popular, is outside the east wall of Jerusalem near the Church of All Nations. The olive trees there are indeed very old, but it is not likely that they go back as far as the time of Christ since the Romans destroyed all the trees in their invasion of Judea in A.D. 70.

The geographical location of the Garden of Gethsemane is not as important as the spiritual message that we receive from what Jesus did there when He accepted "the cup" from His Father's hand. The first Adam rebelled in the Garden of Eden and brought sin and death into the world, but the Last Adam (1 Cor. 15:45) submitted in the Garden of Gethsemane and brought life and salvation for all who will believe.

2. A Costly Cup (22:40-46)

Jesus left eight of His disciples somewhere in the garden and took Peter, James, and John with Him to a private place to pray (Mark 14:32-33). This is the third time He has shared a special occasion with these three men. The first was when Jesus raised Jairus' daughter from the dead (8:41-56), and the second was when He was transfigured before them (9:28-36). There must be a spiritual message here.

Dr. G. Campbell Morgan, the British expositor, has pointed out that each of these occasions had something to do with death. In Jairus' house, Jesus proved Himself to be victorious over death; and on the Mount of Transfiguration, He was glorified through death. (He and Moses and Elijah were talking about His "exodus" in Jerusalem [9:31].) Here in the garden, Jesus was surrendered to death. Since James was the first of the apostles to die (Acts 12:1-2), John the last to die, and Peter experienced great persecution and eventually was crucified, these three lessons were very practical for their own lives.

Jesus was the Son of God and knew full well that He would be raised from the dead, and yet His soul experienced agony as He anticipated what lay before Him. In the hours ahead, He would be humiliated and abused, and suffer shame and pain on the cross. But even more, He would be made sin for us and separated from His Father. He called this solemn experience "drinking the cup." (For parallel uses of this image, see Isa. 51:17, 22; Pss. 73:10 and 75:8; Jer. 25:15-28.)

A comparison of the Gospel accounts reveals that Jesus prayed three times about the cup and returned three times to the disciples, only to find them asleep. How little they realized the testing and danger that lay before them! And how much it would have meant to Jesus to have had their prayer support as He faced Calvary! (See Heb. 5:7-8.)

Dr. Luke is the only Gospel writer who mentions "sweat . . . like great drops of blood." His use of the word *like* may suggest that the sweat merely fell to the ground like clots of blood. But there is a rare physical phenomenon known as *hematidrosis,* in which, under great emotional stress, the tiny blood vessels rupture in the sweat glands and produce a mixture of blood and sweat. The first Adam sinned in a garden and was condemned to living by the sweat of his brow (Gen. 3:19). Jesus, the Last Adam, obeyed the Father in a garden and conquered Adam's sin (Rom. 5:12-21).

Luke is also the only writer to mention the ministry of the angel (v. 43). In fact, both the Gospel of Luke and the Book of Acts give angels a prominent place in the work of the Lord. Angels could not come to die for our sins, but they could strengthen our Saviour as He courageously accepted the cup from His Father's hand. Dr. George Morrison said, "Every life has its Gethsemane, and every Gethsemane has its angel." What an encouragement to God's people when they wrestle and pray about difficult and costly decisions!

3. A Hypocritical Kiss (22:47-48)

Someone has defined "kiss" as "the contraction of the mouth due to the enlargement of the heart." But not all kisses are born out of a loving heart, for kisses can also be deceitful. In the case of Judas, his kiss was the basest kind of hypocrisy and treachery.

It was customary in that day for disciples to greet their teachers with a loving and respectful kiss. Judas used the kiss as a sign to tell the arresting officers who Jesus was (Matt. 26:48-49). Jesus had taught in the temple day after day, and yet the temple guards could not recognize Him!

The presence of such a large group of armed soldiers shows how little Judas really knew about the Lord Jesus. Did he think that Jesus would try to run away or perhaps hide somewhere in the garden? Judas must have expected Jesus and the disciples to resist arrest; otherwise he would not have enlisted so much help. Perhaps he feared that Jesus might perform a miracle, but even if He did, what can a group of armed men do against the power of Almighty God?

Judas was deceitful; he was a liar just like Satan who entered into him (John 13:27 and 8:44). He defiled almost everything that he touched: his name ("Judah" = "praise"), the disciple band (6:13-16), gifts given to Christ (John 12:1-8), and the kiss. He even invaded a private prayer meeting, defiled it with his presence, and betrayed the Saviour *with a kiss.* "Faithful are the wounds of a friend, but the kisses of an enemy are deceitful" (Prov. 27:6).

4. A Useless Sword (22:49-53)

The disciples remembered (and misunderstood) His words about the sword (vv. 35-38), so they asked Him if now was the time to make use of their two swords. Without waiting for the answer, Peter rushed ahead and attacked a man who turned out to be Malchus, a servant to the high priest (John 18:10, 26-27).

Why did Peter do this? For one thing, he had to back up the boastful words he had spoken in the Upper Room (22:33) and again on the way to the garden (Matt. 26:30-35). Peter had been sleeping when he should have been praying, talking when he should have been listening, and boasting when he should have been fearing. Now he was fighting when he should have been surrendering!

Peter made a number of serious mistakes when he attacked Malchus with his sword. To begin with, Peter was fighting the wrong enemy with the wrong weapon. Our enemies are not flesh and blood, and they cannot be defeated with ordinary weapons (Eph. 6:10-18; 2 Cor. 10:3-6). In His wilderness temptations, Jesus defeated Satan with the Word of God (Matt. 4:1-11), and that is the weapon we must use (Heb. 4:12; Eph. 6:17).

Peter also revealed the wrong attitude and trusted the wrong energy. While Jesus was surrendering, Peter was busy declaring war! And he was depending on "the arm of flesh." His whole approach to the situation was not at all Christlike (John 18:36) and stands as a good warning to us today. The lost world may act this way, but it is not the way God's servants should act (2 Tim. 2:24; Matt. 12:19).

It is just like Jesus to act in grace when others are acting in malice (Ps. 103:10). He showed grace to Peter by rebuking his presumptuous sin and repairing the damage he had done. He showed grace to Malchus, a lowly slave, by healing his ear, and He showed grace to the whole world by willingly yielding Himself to the mob and going to Calvary. He did not come to judge but to save (19:10; John 3:17).

Our Lord's last miracle before the cross was not a big flashy thing that attracted attention. It is likely that very few of the men who were there that night even knew what Peter and Jesus had done. Jesus could have summoned twelve legions of angels (Matt. 26:53), one legion (6,000 soldiers) for each of the eleven disciples and one for Himself, but He did not. Instead of performing some spectacular feat, He lovingly healed the ear of an obscure slave and then presented His hands to be bound.

Each of us must decide whether we will go through life *pretending*, like Judas; or *fighting*, like Peter; or *yielding to God's perfect will*, like Jesus. Will it be the kiss, the sword, or the cup?

5. A Crowing Cock (22:54-62)

Our Lord endured six different "trials" before He was condemned to be crucified, three before the Jews and three before the Roman authorities. First, He was taken to Annas, the former high priest who was an influential man in the nation and retained his former title (John 18:12-13). Annas sent Jesus to Caiaphas, his son-in-law, who was the official high priest (Matt. 26:57). Finally, at daybreak, He was tried before the Sanhedrin and found guilty (vv. 66-71).

The Jews did not have the right of capital punishment (John 18:31-32), so they had to take Jesus to the Roman authorities to get Him crucified. First, they took Him to Pilate (23:1-4), who tried to avoid a decision by sending Him to Herod (23:6-12), who sent Him back to Pilate! (23:13-25) When Pilate saw that he could not escape making a decision, he gave the Sanhedrin what they asked for and condemned Jesus to die on a Roman cross.

It was during the second Jewish "trial," the one before Caiaphas, that Peter in the courtyard denied his Lord three times. How did it happen? To begin with, Peter did not take the Lord's warnings seriously (vv. 31-34; Matt. 26:33-35), nor did he "watch and pray" as Jesus had instructed in the garden (Mark 14:37-38). For all of his courage and zeal, the Apostle Peter was totally unprepared for Satan's attacks.

Jesus was led out of the garden, and "Peter followed afar off" (v. 54). This was the next step toward his defeat. In spite of all the sermons that have been delivered on this text, criticizing him for walking at a distance, _Peter was not intended to follow at all._ The "sheep" were supposed to scatter and then meet Jesus later in Galilee (Matt. 26:31). In fact, when He was arrested, Jesus said to the guards, "Let these [disciples] go their way" (John 18:8-9), a clear signal that they were not to follow Him.

Peter and John followed the mob and gained entrance into the courtyard of Caiaphas' house (John 18:15-16). It was a cold night (although Jesus had been sweating!), and Peter first *stood* by the fire (John 18:18) and then *sat down* with the servants and officers (v. 55). Sitting there in enemy territory (Ps. 1:1), Peter was an easy target. While he was thinking only of his own comfort, his Master was being abused by the soldiers (vv. 63-65).

First, it was one of the high priest's servant girls who challenged Peter. She accused him of being with Jesus and of being one of His disciples. Peter lied and said, "Woman, I am not one of His disciples! I don't know Him and I don't know what you are talking about!" He left the fire and went out to the porch (Matt. 26:71), and the cock crowed the first time (Mark 14:68). This in itself should have warned him to get out, but he lingered.

Peter could not escape notice, and a second servant girl told the bystanders, "This man was with Jesus of Nazareth! He is one of them!" For a second time, Peter lied and said, "I am not! I don't know the man!"

The bystanders were not convinced, especially when one of Malchus' relatives showed up and asked, "Didn't I see you in the garden with Him?" Others joined in and said, "Surely you are one of them, because the way you talk gives you away. You talk like a Galilean." (The Galileans had a distinctive dialect.) At this point Peter used an oath and said, "I don't know the man! I don't know what you are talking about!" It was then that the cock crowed for the second time and the Lord's prediction was fulfilled (Mark 14:30).

At that moment, Jesus, being led away to the next trial, turned and looked at Peter; and His look broke Peter's heart. While the bystanders were watching Jesus, Peter slipped out and went off and wept bitterly. It is to Peter's credit that all the Lord had to do was *look* at him to bring him to the place of repentance.

For one cock to crow at the right time while the other birds in the city remained silent was certainly a miracle. But the crowing of the cock was much more than a miracle that fulfilled our Lord's words; it was also a special message to Peter, a message that helped to restore him to fellowship again. What encouragements did the crowing of the cock give to the Apostle Peter?

First, it was an assurance to him that Jesus Christ was still in control of things even though He was a prisoner, bound and seemingly helpless before His captors. Peter could recall witnessing his Lord's authority over the fish, the winds and the waves, and even over disease and death. No matter how dark the hour was for Peter, Jesus was still in control!

Second, the crowing of the cock assured Peter that he could be forgiven. Peter had not been paying close attention to the Word of God. He had argued with it, disobeyed it, and even run ahead of it, but now he "remembered the word of the Lord" (v. 61), and this brought him hope. Why? Because with the word of warning was also a promise of restoration! Peter would be converted and strengthen his brethren (v. 32).

Finally, the miracle of the cock told Peter that a new day was dawning, for after all, that is what the rooster's call means each day. It was not a new day for Judas or for the enemies of the Lord, but it was a new day for Peter as he repented and wept bitterly. "A broken and a contrite heart, O God, thou wilt not despise" (Ps. 51:17). On Resurrection morning, the angel sent a special message to encourage Peter (Mark 16:7), and the Lord Himself appeared to Peter that day and restored him to fellowship (Luke 24:34).

Each one of us, at one time or another, will fail the Lord and then hear (in one way or another) "the crowing of the cock." Satan will tell us that we are finished, that our future has been destroyed, but that is not God's message to us. It was certainly not the end for Peter! His restoration was so complete that he was able to say to the Jews, "But you denied the Holy One and the Just!" (Acts 3:14, NKJV) Peter did not have 1 John 1:9 to read, but he did experience it in his own heart.

6. A Glorious Throne (22:63-71)
Jesus had not yet officially been declared guilty, and yet the soldiers were permitted to mock Him and abuse Him. Here they mocked His claim to being a prophet; later they would mock His claim to being a king (John 19:1-3). But their mockery, sinful as it was, actually fulfilled Christ's own promise (Matt. 20:19). He is an example to us of how we should

behave when sinners ridicule us and our faith (see 1 Peter 2:18-25).

It is generally believed that the Jewish council could not vote on capital offenses at night; so the chief priests, scribes, and elders had to assemble again as soon as it was day. Whether this ruling was in force in our Lord's day, we are not sure, but it does explain the early morning meeting of the Sanhedrin.

This was the climax of the religious trial, and the key issue was, "Is Jesus of Nazareth the Christ of God?" They were sure His claims were false and that He was guilty of blasphemy, and the penalty for blasphemy was death (Lev. 24:10-16).

Jesus knew the hearts of His accusers, their unbelief, and intellectual dishonesty (20:1-8). It was futile to preach a sermon or enter into a debate. They had already rejected the evidence He had given them (John 12:37-43), and more truth would only have increased their responsibility and their judgment (John 9:39-41).

Our Lord called Himself "Son of man," a messianic title found in Daniel 7:13-14. He also claimed to have the right to sit "on the right hand of the power of God" (v. 69), a clear reference to Psalm 110:1, another messianic passage. It was this verse that He quoted earlier that week in His debate with the religious leaders (20:41-44). Jesus saw beyond the sufferings of the cross to the glories of the throne (Heb. 12:2; Phil. 2:1-11).

That our Lord is seated at the right hand of the Father is a truth that is often repeated in the New Testament (Heb. 1:3; 8:1; 10:12; 12:2; 1 Peter 3:22; Acts 2:33; 5:31; 7:55-56; Rom. 8:34; Eph. 1:20; Col. 3:1). This is the place of honor, authority, and power; and by claiming this honor, Jesus was claiming to be God.

Only Luke records the direct question in verse 70 and our Lord's direct answer, which literally was: "You say that I am." They would use this testimony later when they brought Him to Pilate (John 19:7). Some liberal theologians say that Jesus never claimed to be God, and we wonder what they do with this official trial? The Jewish religious leaders knew what Jesus was talking about, and this is why they condemned Him for blasphemy.

The "religious trial" was now over. The next step was to put Him through a civil trial and convince the Roman governor that Jesus of Nazareth was a criminal worthy of death. The Son of God was to be crucified, and only the Romans could do that.

Referring to the Jewish authorities, William Stalker wrote in *The Trial; and Death of Jesus Christ:* "It may be said that they walked according to their light; but the light that was in them was darkness."

"None so blind as those that will not see," wrote Matthew Henry, the noted Bible commentator.

"While you have the light, believe in the light, that you may become sons of light" (John 12:36, NKJV).

11
Condemned and Crucified
Luke 23

The trial and death of Jesus Christ revealed both the wicked heart of man and the gracious heart of God. When men were doing their worst, God was giving His best. "But where sin abounded, grace did much more abound" (Rom. 5:20). Jesus was not crucified because evil men decided to get Him out of the way. His crucifixion was "by the determinate counsel and foreknowledge of God" (Acts 2:23), an appointment made from eternity (1 Peter 1:20; Rev. 13:8).

As you study this chapter, notice the six encounters our Lord experienced during those critical hours.

1. Jesus and Pilate (23:1-25)
Pontius Pilate served as governor of Judea from A.D. 26 to A.D. 36, at which time he was recalled to Rome and then passed out of official Roman history. He was hated by the orthodox Jews and never really understood them. Once he aroused their fury by putting up pagan Roman banners in the Jewish temple, and he was not beneath sending armed spies into the temple to silence Jewish protesters (13:1-3).

In his handling of the trial of Jesus, the governor proved to be indecisive. The Gospel of John records seven different moves that Pilate made as he went *out* to meet the people and then went *in* to question Jesus (John 18:29, 33, 38; 19:1, 4, 9, 13). He kept looking for a loophole, but he found none. Pilate has gone down in history as the man who tried Jesus Christ, three times declared Him not guilty, and yet crucified Him just the same.

Pilate affirming (vv. 1-5). Roman officials were usually up early and at their duties, but Pilate was probably surprised that morning to learn that he had a capital case on his hands, and on Passover at that. The Jewish leaders knew that their religious laws meant nothing to a Roman official, so they emphasized the political aspects of their indictment against Jesus. There were three charges: He perverted the nation, opposed paying the poll tax to Caesar, and claimed to be a king.

Pilate privately interrogated Jesus about His kingship because that was the crucial issue, and he concluded that He was guilty of no crime. Three times during the trial, Pilate clearly affirmed the innocence of Jesus (vv. 4, 14, 22). Dr. Luke reported three other witnesses beside Pilate who also said, "Not guilty!": King Herod (v. 15), one of the malefactors (vv. 40-43), and a Roman centurion (v. 47).

Pilate deferring (vv. 6-12). The Jews rejected his verdict and began to accuse Jesus all the more. When they mentioned Galilee, Pilate, astute politician that he was, immediately saw an opportunity to get Jesus off his hands. He sent Him to Herod Antipas, ruler of Galilee, the man who had murdered John the Baptist, who was anxious to see Jesus (9:7-9). Perhaps the wily king could find some way to please the Jews.

Herod must have been shocked and perhaps nervous when the guards brought Jesus in, but the more he questioned Him, the bolder he became. Perhaps Jesus might even entertain the king with a miracle! In spite of the king's persistent interrogation and the Jews' vehement accusations, Jesus said nothing. *Herod had silenced the voice of God.* It was not Herod who was judging Jesus; it was Jesus who was judging Herod.

The king finally became so bold as to mock Jesus and permit his soldiers to dress Him in "an elegant robe," the kind that was worn by Roman candidates for office. Herod did not issue an official verdict about Jesus (v. 15), but it was clear that he did not find Him guilty of any crime worthy of death (v. 15).

The only thing accomplished by this maneuver was the mending of a broken friendship. Herod was grateful to Pilate for helping him to see Jesus and for honoring him by seeking his counsel. The fact that Herod sent Jesus back to Pilate without issuing a verdict could be interpreted as, "Since we are not in Galilee, Pilate, you have the authority to act, and I will not interfere. Jesus is *your* prisoner, not mine. I know you will do the right thing." Finally, the fact that the two men met over a common threat (or enemy) helped them to put aside their differences and become friends again.

Pilate bargaining (vv. 13-23). He met the Jewish leaders and announced for the second time that he did not find Jesus guilty of the charges they had made against Him. The fact that Herod backed Pilate's decision would not have impressed the Jews very much, because they despised Herod almost as much as they despised the Romans.

Since it was customary at Passover for the governor to release a prisoner, Pilate offered the Jews a compromise: he would chastise Jesus and let Him go. He had another prisoner on hand, Barabbas, but Pilate was sure the Jews would not want him to be released. After all, Barabbas was a robber (John 18:40), a murderer, and an insurrectionist (v. 19). He may have been a leader of the Jewish Zealots who at that time was working for the overthrow of Rome.

We must not think that the general populace of the city was gathered before Pilate and crying out for the blood of Jesus, although a curious crowd no doubt gathered. It was primarily the official religious leaders of the nation, the chief priests in particular (v. 23), who shouted Pilate down and told him to crucify Jesus. To say that the people who cried "Hosanna!" on Palm Sunday ended up crying "Crucify Him!" on Good Friday is not completely accurate.

Pilate yielding (vv. 24-25). Pilate realized that his mishandling of the situation had almost caused a riot, and a Jewish uprising was the last thing he wanted during Passover. So, he called for water and washed his hands before the crowd, affirming his innocence (Matt. 27:24-25). He was a compromiser who was "willing to content the people" (Mark 15:15). Barabbas was released and Jesus was condemned to die on a Roman cross.

Pilate was a complex character. He openly said that Jesus was innocent, yet he permitted Him to be beaten and condemned Him to die. He carefully questioned Jesus and even trembled at His answers, but the truth of the Word did not make a difference in his decisions. He wanted to be popular and not right; he was more concerned about reputation than he was character. If Herod had silenced the voice of God, then Pilate smothered the voice of God. He had his opportunity and wasted it.

2. Jesus and Simon (23:26)

It was a part of the prisoner's humiliation that he carry his own cross to the place of execution, so when Jesus left Pilate's hall, He was carrying either the cross or the crossbeam (John 19:17). Apparently, He was unable to go on, for the soldiers had to "draft" Simon of Cyrene to carry the cross for Him. (This was a legal Roman procedure. See Matt. 5:41.) When you consider all that Jesus had endured since His arrest in the garden, it is not difficult to imagine Him falling under the load. But there is something more involved: carrying the cross was a sign of guilt, *and our Lord was not guilty!*

Thousands of Jews came to Jerusalem from other nations to celebrate the feasts (Acts 2:5-11), and Simon was among them. He had traveled over 800 miles from Africa to celebrate Passover, and now he was being humiliated on a most holy day! What would he say to his family when he got home?

What looked to Simon like a catastrophe turned out to be a wonderful opportunity, for it brought him in contact with Jesus Christ. (By the way, where was the *other* Simon—Simon Peter—who had promised Jesus to go with Him to prison and to death?) Simon may have come into the city to attend the 9 o'clock prayer meeting in the temple, but the soldiers rearranged his schedule for him.

We have good reason to believe that Simon was converted because of this encounter with Jesus. Mark identified him as "the father of Alexander and Rufus" (Mark 15:21), two men that Mark assumed his Roman readers would know. A Christian named Rufus was greeted by Paul in Romans 16:13, and it is possible that he was the son of Simon of Cyrene. Apparently Simon and his two sons became well-known Christians who were held in honor in the church.

Before Simon met Jesus, he had religion and devotion; but after he met Jesus, he had reality and salvation. He did both a physical and spiritual "about face" that morning, and it transformed his life. God can still use unexpected and difficult situations, even humiliating situations, to bring people to the Saviour.

3. Jesus and the Jerusalem Women (23:27-31)
Public executions drew crowds of spectators, and one involving Jesus would especially attract attention. Add to this the fact that Jerusalem was crowded with pilgrims, and it is not

difficult to believe that a "great multitude" was following the
condemned men to Calvary.

In that crowd was a group of women who openly wept and
lamented as they sympathized with Jesus and contemplated
the terrible spiritual condition of their nation. It has been
pointed out that, as far as the Gospel records are concerned,
no woman was ever an enemy of Jesus. Nor was Jesus ever
the enemy of womankind. His example, His teachings, and
most of all, His redemption have done much to dignify and
elevate women. The news of His birth was shared with a
Jewish maiden, His death was witnessed by grieving women,
and the good news of His resurrection was announced first to
a woman who had been demon-possessed.

Jesus appreciated their sympathy and used it to teach them
and us an important lesson. While they were weeping over
the injustice of *one man's death*, He was looking ahead and
grieving over the terrible destruction of *the entire nation*, a
judgment that was wholly justified (see 19:41-44). Alas, it
would be the women and children who would suffer the
most, a fact supported by history. The Romans attempted to
starve the Jews into submission; and hungry men, defending
their city, took food from their suffering wives and children
and even killed and ate their own flesh and blood.

The nation of Israel was like a "green tree" during the years
when Jesus was on earth. It was a time of blessing and opportunity, and it should have been a time of fruitfulness. But the
nation rejected Him and became like a "dry tree," fit only for
the fire. Jesus often would have gathered His people together,
but they would not. In condemning Him, they only condemned themselves.

We might paraphrase His words, "If the Roman authorities
do this to One who is innocent, what will they do to you who
are guilty? When the day of judgment arrives, can there be
any escape for you?"

4. Jesus and the Malefactors (23:32-43)

It had been prophecied that the Suffering Servant would be "numbered with the transgressors" (22:37; Isa. 53:12), and two criminals were crucified with Jesus, men who were robbers (Matt. 27:38). The Greek word means "one who uses violence to rob openly," in contrast to the thief who secretly enters a house and steals. These two men may have been guilty of armed robbery involving murder.

The name *Calvary* comes from the Latin *calvaria* which means "a skull." (The Greek is *kranion*, which gives us the English word *cranium*, and the Aramaic word is *Golgotha*.) The name is not explained in the New Testament. The site may have resembled a skull, as does "Gordon's Calvary" near the Damascus Gate in Jerusalem. Or perhaps the name simply grew out of the ugly facts of execution.

Our Lord was crucified about 9 A.M. and remained on the cross until 3 P.M.; and from noon to 3 P.M., there was darkness over all the land (Mark 15:25, 33). Jesus spoke seven times during those six terrible hours:

1. "Father, forgive them" (23:34).
2. "Today shalt thou be with Me in paradise" (23:43).
3. "Woman, behold thy son" (John 19:25-27).
   [Three hours of darkness; Jesus is silent]
4. "Why hast Thou forsaken Me?" (Matt. 27:46)
5. "I thirst" (John 19:28).
6. "It is finished!" (John 19:30)
7. "Father, into Thy hands" (23:46).

Luke recorded only three of these seven statements, the first, the second, and the last. Our Lord's prayer for His enemies, and His ministry to a repentant thief, fit in well with Luke's purpose to show Jesus Christ as the sympathetic Son of man who cared for the needy.

While they were nailing Him to the cross, He repeatedly prayed, "Father, forgive them; for they know not what they do" (v. 34). Not only was He practicing what He taught (6:27-28), but He was fulfilling prophecy and making "intercession for the transgressors" (Isa. 53:12).

We must not infer from His prayer that ignorance is a basis for forgiveness, or that those who sinned against Jesus were automatically forgiven because He prayed. Certainly both the Jews and the Romans were ignorant of the *enormity* of their sin, but that could not absolve them. The Law provided a sacrifice for sins committed ignorantly, but there was no sacrifice for deliberate presumptuous sin (Num. 15:27-31; Ex. 21:14; Ps. 51:16-17). Our Lord's intercession postponed God's judgment on the nation for almost forty years, giving them additional opportunities to be saved (Acts 3:17-19).

It was providential that Jesus was crucified *between* the two thieves, for this gave both of them equal access to the Saviour. Both could read Pilate's superscription, "This is Jesus of Nazareth the king of the Jews," and both could watch Him as He graciously gave His life for the sins of the world.

The one thief imitated the mockery of the religious leaders and asked Jesus to rescue him from the cross, but the other thief had different ideas. He may have reasoned, "If this man is indeed the Christ, and if He has a kingdom, and if He has saved others, then He can meet my greatest need which is salvation from sin. I am not ready to die!" It took courage for this thief to defy the influence of his friend and the mockery of the crowd, and it took faith for him to trust a dying King! When you consider all that he had to overcome, the faith of this thief is astounding.

The man was saved wholly by grace; it was the gift of God (Eph. 2:8-9). He did not deserve it and he could not earn it. His salvation was personal and secure, guaranteed by the Word of Jesus Christ. The man hoped for some kind of help in the future, but Jesus gave him forgiveness that very day, and he died and went with Jesus to paradise (2 Cor. 12:1-4).

It should be noted that the people at Calvary fulfilled Old Testament prophecy in what they did: gambling for our Lord's clothing (Ps. 22:18), mocking Him (Ps. 22:6-8), and offering Him vinegar to drink (Ps. 69:21). God was still on the throne and His Word was still in control.

5. Jesus and the Father (23:44-49)

We must keep in mind that what our Lord accomplished on the cross was an eternal transaction that involved Him and the Father. He did not die as a martyr who had failed in a lost cause. Nor was He only an example for people to follow. Isaiah 53 makes it clear that Jesus did not die for His own sins, because He had none; He died for our sins. He made His soul an offering for sin (Isa. 53:4-6, 10-12).

The three hours of darkness was a miracle. It was not an eclipse, because that would have been impossible during the Passover season when there is a full moon. It was a God-sent darkness that shrouded the cross as the Son of God was made sin for us (2 Cor. 5:21). It was as though all nature was sympathizing with the Creator as He suffered and died. When Israel was in Egypt, three days of darkness preceded the first Passover (Ex. 10:21ff). When Jesus was on the cross, three hours of darkness preceded the death of God's Lamb for the sins of the world (John 1:29).

Both Matthew (27:45-46) and Mark (15:33-34) record our Lord's cry at the close of the darkness, a Hebrew quotation from Psalm 22:1, "My God, My God, why hast Thou forsaken Me?" What this abandonment was and how Jesus felt it are not explained to us, but certainly it involves the fact that He became sin for us.

Our Lord cried with a loud voice, "It is finished!" (John 19:30) a declaration of victory. He had finished the work the

Father gave Him to do (John 17:4). The work of redemption was completed, the types and prophecies were fulfilled (Heb. 9:24ff), and the Saviour could now rest.

He then addressed His Father in the final statement from the cross, "Father, into Thy hands I commend My spirit" (Ps. 31:5). This was actually a bedtime prayer used by Jewish children, and it tells us how our Lord died: confidently, willingly (John 10:17-18), and victoriously. Those who know Jesus as their Saviour may die with the same confidence and assurance (Phil. 1:20-23; 2 Cor. 5:1-8).

When our Lord released His spirit, the veil of the temple was torn in two "from the top to the bottom" (Mark 15:38). This miracle announced to the priests and people that the way into God's presence was open for all who would come to Him by faith through Jesus Christ (Heb. 9:1–10:25). No more do sinners need earthly temples, altars, sacrifices, or priests, for all had now been fulfilled in the finished work of the Son of God.

Luke recorded three responses to the events of the last moments of Christ's death. The centurion who was in charge of the execution testified, "Certainly this was a righteous [innocent] man, the Son of God" (v. 47; Mark 15:39). He was greatly impressed by the darkness, the earthquake (Matt. 27:54), and certainly the way Jesus suffered and died. He must have been shocked when Jesus shouted and then instantly died, for victims of crucifixion often lingered for days and did not have the strength to speak.

The people who came to "see the spectacle" began to drift away one by one, some of them beating their breasts as they felt their guilt (18:13). Were these people believers? Probably not. They were spectators who were attracted to the execution, but certainly they saw and heard enough to convict them of their own sins.

Finally, our Lord's friends were there, including the women

who followed Jesus (8:1-3; 24:22). It is significant that the women were the last at the cross and the first at the tomb on Easter morning.

6. Jesus and Joseph of Arimathea (23:50-56)

Joseph and his friend Nicodemus (John 19:38-42) were both members of the Jewish council, but they had not been present to vote against Jesus. Mark 14:64 states that the whole council condemned Him, and that could not have happened if Joseph and Nicodemus had been there.

It is likely that Joseph and Nicodemus had learned from the Old Testament Scriptures how Jesus would die, so they agreed to take care of His burial. The new tomb was likely Joseph's, prepared in a garden near Golgotha but not for himself; it was for Jesus. No rich man would prepare his own burial place so near a place of execution and so far from his own home. The two men could well have been hiding in the tomb while Jesus was on the cross, waiting for that moment when He would yield up His life. They would have the spices and the winding sheets all prepared, for they would probably not be able to go shopping for these items on Passover.

When Jesus died, Joseph immediately went to Pilate for permission to have the body, and Nicodemus stayed at Calvary to keep watch. They tenderly took Jesus from the cross, quickly carried Him to the garden, washed the body, and wrapped it with the spices. It was a temporary burial; they would return after the Sabbath to do the job properly. When they laid Jesus into the new tomb, they fulfilled Isaiah 53:9, and they kept the Romans from throwing His body on the garbage dump outside the city. Condemned criminals lost the right to proper burial, but God saw to it that His Son's body was buried with dignity and love.

It was important that the body be buried properly, for God would raise Jesus from the dead. If there were any doubt about His death or burial, that could affect the message and the ministry of the Gospel (1 Cor. 15:1-8).

When after six days God finished the work of the "old creation," He rested (Gen. 2:1-3). After six hours, our Lord finished the work of the "new creation" (2 Cor. 5:17), and He rested on the Sabbath in Joseph's tomb.

But that was not the end of the story.

He would rise again!

12

The Son of Man Triumphs!

Luke 24

"Christianity is in its very essence a resurrection religion," says Dr. John Stott. "The concept of resurrection lies at its heart. If you remove it, Christianity is destroyed."

The resurrection of Jesus Christ affirms to us that He is indeed the Son of God, just as He claimed to be (Rom. 1:4). It also proves that His sacrifice for sin has been accepted and that the work of salvation is completed (Rom. 4:24-25). Those who trust Him can "walk in newness of life" because He is alive and imparts His power to them (Rom. 6:4; Gal. 2:20). Our Lord's resurrection also declares to us that He is the Judge who will come one day and judge the world (Acts 17:30-31).

It is no surprise, then, that Satan has attacked the truth of the Resurrection. The first lie that he spawned was that the disciples came and stole Christ's body (Matt. 28:11-15), but it is difficult to imagine how they could have done this. To begin with, the tomb was carefully guarded (Matt. 27:61-66); and it would have been next to impossible for the frightened apostles to overpower the soldiers, open the tomb and secure the body. But the biggest obstacle is the fact that the apostles themselves *did not believe that He would be resurrected!* Why, then, would they steal His body and try to perpetrate a hoax?

A second lie is that Jesus did not really die on the cross but only swooned, and when He was put into the cool tomb, He revived. But Pilate carefully checked with the centurion to see whether Jesus was dead (Mark 15:44), and the Roman soldiers who broke the legs of the two thieves knew that Jesus had died (John 19:31-34). Furthermore, how could a "cool tomb" transform Christ's body so that He could appear and disappear and walk through closed doors?

The message of the Gospel rests upon the death of Jesus Christ *and His resurrection* (1 Cor. 15:1-8). The apostles were sent out as witnesses of His resurrection (Acts 1:22), and the emphasis in the Book of Acts is on the resurrection of Jesus Christ.

This explains why Luke climaxed his book with a report of some of the appearances of Jesus after He had been raised from the dead. He first appeared to Mary Magdalene (John 20:11-18), then to the "other women" (Matt. 28:9-10), and then to the two men on the way to Emmaus (24:13-22). At some time, He also appeared to Peter (24:34) and to His half-brother James (1 Cor. 15:7).

That evening, He appeared to the apostles (24:36-43), but Thomas was not with them (John 20:19-25). A week later, He appeared to the apostles again, especially for the sake of Thomas (John 20:26-31). He appeared to seven of the apostles when they were fishing at the Sea of Galilee (John 21). He appeared several times to the apostles before His ascension, teaching them and preparing them for their ministry (Acts 1:1-12).

When the believers discovered that Jesus was alive, it made a tremendous difference in their lives.

1. Perplexed Hearts: He Opens the Tomb (24:1-12)

We do not know at what time Jesus arose from the dead on the first day of the week, but it must have been very early. The earthquake and the angel (Matt. 28:2-4) opened the tomb, not to let Jesus out but to let the witnesses in. "Come and see, go and tell!" is the Easter mandate for the church.

Mary Magdalene had been especially helped by Jesus and was devoted to Him (8:2). She had lingered at the cross (Mark 15:47), and then she was first at the tomb. With her were Mary the mother of James; Joanna; and other devout women (v. 10), hoping to finish preparing their Lord's body for burial. It was a sad labor of love that was transformed into gladness when they discovered that Jesus was alive.

"Who will roll the stone away?" was their main concern. The Roman soldiers would not break the Roman seal, especially for a group of mourning Jewish women. But God had solved the problem for them; the tomb was open *and there was no body to prepare!*

At this point two angels appeared on the scene. Matthew (28:2) and Mark (16:5) mention only one of the two, the one who gave the message to the women. There was a kind rebuke in his message as he reminded them of their bad memories! More than once, Jesus had told His followers that He would suffer and die and be raised from the dead (Matt. 16:21; 17:22-23; 20:17-19; Luke 9:22, 44; 18:31-34). How sad it is when God's people forget His Word and live defeated lives. Today, the Spirit of God assists us to remember His Word (John 14:26).

Obedient to their commission, the women ran to tell the disciples the good news, but the men did not believe them! (According to Mark 16:14, Jesus later rebuked them for their unbelief.) Mary Magdalene asked Peter and John to come to examine the tomb (John 20:1-10), and they too saw the proof that Jesus was not there. However, all that the evidence said was that the body was gone and that apparently there had been no violence.

As Mary lingered by the tomb weeping, Jesus Himself ap-peared to her (John 20:11-18). It is one thing to see the empty tomb and the empty graveclothes, but quite something else to meet the risen Christ. We today cannot see the evidence in the tomb, but we do have the testimony of the witnesses found in the inspired Word of God. And we can live out our faith in Jesus Christ and know *personally* that He is alive in us (Gal. 2:20).

Keep in mind that these women did not expect to see Jesus alive. They had forgotten His resurrection promises and went to the tomb only to finish anointing His body. To say that they had hallucinations and only thought they saw Jesus is to fly in the face of the evidence. And would this many people halluci-nate about the same thing at the same time? Not likely. They became excited witnesses, even to their leaders, that Jesus Christ is alive!

2. Discouraged Hearts: He Opens Their Eyes (24:13-35)

Emmaus was a small village eight miles northwest of Jerusa-lem. The two men walking from Jerusalem to Emmaus were discouraged disciples who had no reason to be discouraged. They had heard the reports of the women that the tomb was empty and that Jesus was alive, but they did not believe them. They had hoped that Jesus would redeem Israel (v. 21), but their hopes had been shattered. We get the impression that these men were discouraged and disappointed because God did not do what they wanted Him to do. They saw the glory of the kingdom, but they failed to understand the suffering.

Jesus graciously walked with them and listened to their "animated heated conversation" (v. 17, ET). No doubt they were quoting various Old Testament prophecies and trying to remember what Jesus had taught, but they were unable to put it all together and come up with an explanation that made sense. Was He a failure or a success? Why did He have to die? Was there a future for the nation?

There is a touch of humor in verse 19 when Jesus asked, "What things?" *He had been at the heart of all that had happened in Jerusalem, and now He was asking them to tell Him what occurred!* How patient our Lord is with us as He listens to us tell Him what He already knows (Rom. 8:34). But we may come "boldly" ("with freedom of speech") to His throne and pour out our hearts to Him, and He will help us (Heb. 4:16; Ps. 62:8).

The longer Cleopas talked, the more he indicted himself and his friend for their unbelief. What more evidence could they want? Witnesses (including apostles) had seen the tomb empty. Angels had announced that Jesus was alive. Witnesses had seen Him alive and heard Him speak. The proof was there!

"Faith comes by hearing, and hearing by the word of God" (Rom. 10:17, NKJV). This explains why Jesus opened the Word to these two men as the three of them walked to Emmaus. Their real problem was not in their heads but in their hearts (see vv. 25 and 32, and note v. 38). They could have discussed the subject for days and never arrived at a satisfactory answer. What they needed was a fresh understanding of the Word of God, and Jesus gave that understanding to them. He opened the Scriptures and then opened their eyes, and they realized that Jesus was not only alive *but right there with them!*

What was their basic problem? They did not believe all that the prophets had written about the Messiah. That was the problem with most of the Jews in that day: they saw Messiah as a conquering Redeemer, but they did not see Him as a Suffering Servant. As they read the Old Testament, they saw the glory but not the suffering, the crown but not the cross.

The teachers in that day were not unlike some of the "success preachers" today, blind to the *total* message of the Bible.

That was some Bible conference, and I wish I could have been there! Imagine the greatest Teacher explaining the greatest themes from the greatest Book and bringing the greatest blessings to men's lives: eyes open to see Him, hearts open to receive the Word, and lips open to tell others what Jesus said to them!

Perhaps Jesus started at Genesis 3:15, the first promise of the Redeemer, and traced that promise through the Scriptures. He may have lingered at Genesis 22, which tells of Abraham placing his only beloved son on the altar. Surely He touched on Passover, the levitical sacrifices, the tabernacle ceremonies, the Day of Atonement, the serpent in the wilderness, the Suffering Servant in Isaiah 53, and the prophetic messages of Psalms 22 and 69. *The key to understanding the Bible is to see Jesus Christ on every page.* He did not teach them only doctrine or prophecy; He taught "the things concerning Himself" (v. 27).

These men had talked to Jesus and listened to Jesus, and when He made as though He would go on alone, they asked Jesus to come home with them. *They had been won by the Word of God,* and they did not even know who the stranger was. All they knew was that their hearts were "burning" within them, and they wanted the blessing to last.

The more we receive the Word of God, the more we will want to fellowship with the God of the Word. The hymn writer expressed it perfectly: "Beyond the sacred page/I seek Thee, Lord." Understanding Bible knowledge can lead to a "big head" (1 Cor. 8:1), but receiving Bible truth and walking with the Saviour will lead to a burning heart.

Jesus opened the Scriptures to them, and then He opened their eyes so that they recognized Him. *Now they knew for themselves that Jesus was alive.* They had the evidence of the open tomb, the angels, the witnesses, the Scriptures and now their own personal experience with the Lord. The fact that Jesus vanished did not mean that He abandoned them, for He was with them even though they could not see Him; and they would see Him again.

The best evidence that we have understood the Bible and met the living Christ is that we have something exciting to share with others. The two men immediately left Emmaus and returned to Jerusalem to tell the believers that they had met Jesus. But when they arrived, the apostles and the others *told them* that Jesus was alive and had appeared to Peter! What a difference it would make in our church services if everybody who gathers would come to tell about meeting the living Christ! If our services are "dead" it is probably because we are not really walking with and listening to the living Saviour.

The "breaking of bread" (vv. 30, 35) refers to a meal and not to the Lord's Supper. As far as we know, the apostles were the only ones Jesus had instructed about the Lord's Supper; and it was not likely that our Lord would celebrate it at this time. Jesus revealed Himself to them during a common meal, and that is often how He works. We must learn to see Him in the everyday things of life. However, as we do celebrate the Lord's Supper from time to time, we want Jesus to reveal Himself to us in a new way, and we must not be satisfied with anything less.

3. Troubled Hearts: He Opens Their Minds (24:36-46)
So many exciting things had happened that day and so much was unexplained that ten of the apostles, plus other believers, met together that evening and shared their witness with one another. While Cleopas and his friend were telling their story, *Jesus Himself appeared in the room!* And the doors were shut! (John 20:19)

You would have expected the believers to heave a great sigh of relief and sing a hymn of praise, but instead they became terrified, frightened, and troubled (vv. 37-38). They thought a ghost had appeared! It all happened so suddenly that they were totally unprepared, even though several of them had already seen the risen Christ. Mark 16:14 suggests that the condition of their hearts had something to do with the expression of their fears.

Jesus sought to calm them. The first thing He did was to give them His blessing: "Peace be unto you!" He even repeated the blessing (John 20:19-21). "The God of peace" had raised Jesus from the dead, and there was nothing for them to fear (Heb. 13:20-21). Because of His sacrifice on the cross, men and women could now have peace with God (Rom. 5:1) and enjoy the peace of God (Phil. 4:6-7).

The next thing He did to calm them was to show them His wounded hands and feet (Ps. 22:16) and assure them that He was not a ghost. Songwriters sometimes mention His "scars," but the record says nothing about "scars." The "prints" of Calvary were on His glorified body (John 20:24-29), and they are still there (Rev. 5:6, 9, 12). It has well been said that the only work of man now in heaven is the marks of Calvary on the body of the exalted Saviour.

Jesus even ate some honey and fish to prove to His doubting followers that He was indeed alive and real, and He even invited them to *feel* His body (v. 39; 1 John 1:1). With our limited knowledge, we cannot explain how a human body can be solid flesh and bones and still pass through closed doors and appear and disappear, or how it can be glorified and still carry the marks of the cross. We do know that we shall one day be like Him and share His glory (1 John 3:1-2).

Verse 41 describes a perplexing emotion: "they believed not for joy." It was just too good to be true! Jacob had this same feeling when he got the news that Joseph was alive (Gen.

45:26-28), and the nation of Israel experienced it when God gave them a great deliverance (Ps. 126:1-3). Jesus had told His disciples that they would rejoice when they saw Him again, and the promise was fulfilled (John 16:22).

The final source of peace and assurance is the Word of God, so our Lord "opened their understanding" of the Old Testament Scriptures, just as He had done with the Emmaus disciples. After all, the believers were not being sent into the world to share their own personal experiences but to share the truths of the Word of God. We today cannot touch and feel the Lord Jesus, nor is it necessary that we do so; but we can rest our faith on the Word of God (1 John 1:1-5).

Jesus not only enabled them to understand the Law, the Prophets, and the Psalms, but He also reminded them of what He had taught them, and He explained how it all fit together. Now they began to understand the necessity for His suffering and death and how the cross related to the promise of the kingdom (see 1 Peter 1:10-12). What a privilege it was for them to listen to Jesus expound the Word!

4. Joyful Hearts: He Opens Their Lips (24:47-53)

But privilege always brings responsibility; they were to be witnesses of all that He had said and done (Acts 1:8). A witness is somebody who sincerely tells what he has seen and heard (Acts 4:20), and the word *witness* is used in one way or another twenty-nine times in the Book of Acts. As Christians, we are not judges or prosecuting attorneys sent to condemn the world. We are witnesses who point to Jesus Christ and tell lost sinners how to be saved.

How could a group of common people ever hope to fulfill that kind of a commission? God promised to provide the power (v. 49; Acts 1:8), and He did. On the Day of Pentecost, the Holy Spirit came upon the church and empowered them to preach the Word (Acts 2). After Pentecost, the Spirit continued to fill them with great power (see Acts 4:33).

Witnessing is not something that we do for the Lord; it is something that He does through us, *if* we are filled with the Holy Spirit. There is a great difference between a "sales talk" and a Spirit-empowered witness. "People do not come to Christ at the end of an argument," said Vance Havner. "Simon Peter came to Jesus because Andrew went after him with a testimony." We go forth in the authority of His name, in the power of His spirit, heralding His Gospel of His grace.

Verses 50-52 should be compared with Mark 16:19-20 and Acts 1:9-12. For some reason, our Lord's ascension is not given the prominence in the church that it deserves. Think of what it meant to Him to return to heaven and sit upon the throne of glory! (John 17:5, 11) His ascension is proof that He has conquered every enemy and and that He reigns supremely "far above all" (Eph. 1:18-23).

In heaven today, our Lord ministers as our High Priest (Heb. 7:25) and our Advocate (1 John 2:1). As High Priest, He gives us the grace we need to face testing and temptation (Heb. 4:14-16); and if we fail, as Advocate He forgives and restores us when we confess our sins (1 John 1:6-10). As the glorified Head of the church, Jesus Christ is equipping His people to live for Him and serve Him in this present world (Heb. 13:20-21; Eph. 4:7-16). Through the Word of God and prayer, He is ministering to us by His Spirit and making us more like Himself.

Of course, He is also preparing in heaven a home for His people (John 14:1-6), and one day He will return and take us to be with Him forever.

The last thing our Lord did was to bless His people, and the first thing they did was to worship Him! The two always go together, for as we truly worship Him, He will share His blessings. He not only opened their lips to witness, but He also opened their lips to worship and praise Him!

Dr. Luke opened his Gospel with a scene in the temple (1:8ff), and he closed his Gospel the same way (v. 53). But what a contrast between the unbelieving, silent priest and the trusting, joyful saints! Luke has explained how Jesus went to Jerusalem and accomplished the work of redemption. His book begins and ends in Jerusalem. But his next book, The Acts of the Apostles, would explain how that Gospel traveled from Jerusalem to Rome!

Is the Gospel going out to the ends of the earth from your Jerusalem?